THE BATTLE DISCOVERY GLOSSARY OF

PEARL HARBOR

DECEMBER 7, 1941

Originally published as *The Lampion Glossary of Pearl Harbor.*

Stone Tower Press
7 Ellen Rd.
Middletown, RI 02842

Cover illustration: The USS *Arizona* (BB-39) burning after the Japanese attack on Pearl Harbor. Government photograph NARA 195617

ISBN: 979-8-9868172-1-7

Formatting and cover design by Amy Cole, JPL Design Solutions
Maps by Dr. Gina Palmer
Special thanks to Dr. Stanley M. Carpenter.

Printed in the United States of America

To Douglas V. Smith, Ph.D.

Professor Emeritus, U.S. Naval War College

Friend, Mentor, Naval Aviator, Historian

CONTENTS

Introduction 1

A to Z Entries 3

Appendices 173

It's All in a Name:
Allied Identification of Japanese Planes 173

Aircraft Recognition Chart 175

Japanese Air Attacks 176

Pearl Harbor Anchorage at Time of the Attack........177

Recommended Reading 179

About the Authors 181

INTRODUCTION

The following pages are intended to provide a quick-reference guide to more than 300 ships, planes, people, and units involved in the Japanese attack of Oahu and Pearl Harbor on December 7, 1941. Due to limitations in the scope of the volume, not every unit involved on that historic day is represented. However, it is hoped that this book will be a useful reference guide to some of the major aspects of the attack.

BATTLE
• DISCOVERY •
GLOSSARY

A to Z ENTRIES

USS *Arizona* burning with her superstructure leaning over the shattered forward hull after being torn open by the explosion of the forward magazine.

(U.S. Navy History and Heritage Command photo)

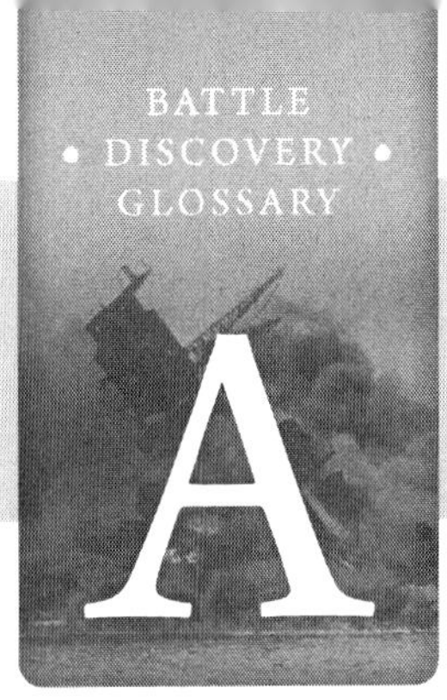

"a date which will live in infamy"

The phrase "a date which will live in infamy" is the amost famous phrase from the seven-minute "Infamy Speech," a speech delivered by President Franklin D. Roosevelt to a Joint Session of Congress on December 8, 1941. The speech described the Japanese attack on U.S. forces at Pearl Harbor, Hawaii. It was broadcast live by radio and attracted the largest audience in U.S. radio history with more than 81% of American households listening to it. The famous phrase is often misquoted as "a day" rather than "a date," however, Roosevelt intentionally chose the word "date" wanting to emphasize December 7, 1941 rather the day of the attack which was a Sunday.

Abukuma

The Japanese *Nagara*-class light cruiser *Abukuma* was named after the Abukuma River and commissioned in May 1925. It served as the flagship of Rear Admiral Omori's Destroyer Squadron 1 consisting of *Shiranui, Arare, Kagerō, Kasumi, Tanikaze, Hamakaze, Isokaze,* and *Urakaze.* It was sunk in October 1944 during the Battle of Suriago Strait.

Aichi D3A/3A1 Type 99

The Aichi D3A/3A1 Type 99 aircraft (abbreviated "*kanbaku*"), was code named by Allied intelligence as "Val." It was the primary dive bomber of the Imperial Japanese Navy (IJN) and sank more Allied warship tonnage than any other Axis aircraft in the war. It was a carrier-borne, single engine-dive bomber with 1 250-kg (551-lb) bomb under the fuselage and 1 60-kg (132-lb) bomb under each wing. Speed of 242 mph (389 kph), range of 915 miles (1473 km), service ceiling of 30,500 ft (9,300 m) and a crew of two (pilot and gunner). The priority of their ship targets during the attack was U.S. aircraft carriers if they were in port and cruisers. Fifty-one participated in the First Wave and 78 in the Second Wave Some sources say there were 54 and 81 but discrepancy may come from the fact that 1 from *Kaga* was unable to take off and 2 were forced to return with engine trouble. First wave targets included aircraft at Wheeler Field, Hickam Field, and the seaplane base at Ford Island. Second Wave targets were ships including *Pennsylvania* and *Nevada.* A total of 15 were lost.

Aichi E131A Type 0

The Aichi E131A Type 0 aircraft was code named by Allied intelligence as "Jake," was a long-range reconnaissance floatplane. It served as a weather and scout plane during the attack.

Aiea Bay

See Pearl Harbor.

"Air raid Pearl Harbor. This is no drill."

This was a phrase used in a naval message ordered sent at 0758 to "all ships present at Hawaiin [sic] area" by Lieutenant Commander Logan C. Ramsay, USN the Operations Officer of Patrol Wing Two after watching a low-flying Japanese plane drop a bomb on Ford Island. In his testimony before a Joint Committee of Congress investigating the attack he stated that after seeing a bomb detonate: "I dashed across the hall into the radio room, ordered a broadcast in plain English on all frequencies, 'Air Raid, Pearl Harbor. This is no drill.' The detonation of the bomb dropped by that first plane was my first positive knowledge of an enemy attack."

Aircraft carriers (Japanese)

There were 6 carriers that participated in the attack (*Akagi, Kaga, Hiryū, Shōkaku, Sōryū, Zuikaku*).

Aircraft carriers (United States)

On the day of the attack, the U.S. had 7 carriers (*Enterprise, Hornet, Lexington, Ranger, Saratoga, Wasp,* and *Yorktown*) and 1 aircraft escort vessel (*Long Island*) in commission. Three of these (*Enterprise, Lexington,* and *Saratoga*) were assigned to the Pacific Fleet but none of them were in port at the time of the attack.

Akagi

The Japanese aircraft carrier *Akagi* ("Red Castle") was initially laid down as an *Amagi*-class battlecruiser but was converted to an aircraft carrier while under construction to comply with terms of the Washington Naval Treaty (1922). It was named after Mount Akagi and commissioned in 1927 with a refit from 1935–1938. *Akagi* had a length of 857 ft. It was 1 of 6 Japanese carriers that participated in the attack (*Akagi, Kaga, Hiryū, Shōkaku, Sōryū, Zuikaku*). It carried 21 Mitsubishi A6M "Zero," 18 Aichi D3A "Val," and 27 Nakajima B5N "Kate" aircraft and launched them from 230 nautical miles from Pearl Harbor. One of its First Wave Zeros was shot down. *Akagi* was commanded by Captain Kiichi Hasegawa and was Vice Admiral Nagumo's flagship for the striking force attacking Pearl Harbor. *Akagi* was damaged by U.S. aircraft during the Battle of Midway, scuttled, and sunk on June 5, 1942.

Akebono

The *Akebono* was the Imperial Japanese Navy (IJN) destroyer that sailed with the Pearl Harbor Strike Force but was assigned to bombard Midway Island. It was sunk by aircraft from Task Force 38 in Manila Bay on November 13, 1944.

Akigumo

Akigumo ("Autumn Clouds"), was a Japanese *Kagerō*-class destroyer commissioned in September 1941. It served as part of the Scouting Group of Rear Admiral Omori that accompanied Vice Admiral Nagumo's Strike Force. Later in the war it was torpedoed and sunk in April 1944 by the submarine USS *Redfin* 30 miles southeast of Zamboana.

Allen (DD-66)

The destroyer USS *Allen* was moored in the East Loch to *Chew, Solace* nearby to port, berth X-5, and undamaged by the attack. The *Sampson*-class destroyer was originally commissioned in 1917 and served on escort duty and U-boat patrols during the First World War. In 1928 it returned to the Reserve Fleet and was berthed in Philadelphia, remaining there until being re-commissioned in 1940 and eventually joining the Pacific Fleet as a unit of Destroyer Division 80 and moving with the fleet from the west coast of the U.S. to Pearl Harbor. After the attack *Allen* served on patrol and escort duty near the Hawaiian Islands and made routine round-trips to the west coast of the U.S. throughout the war.

Antares (AKS-3)

The stores issue ship USS *Antares*, operating at the harbor entrance was undamaged and docked at Honolulu at 1146. The first of its class, *Antares* was commissioned in February 1922. Originally classified as a "miscellaneous auxillary" ship, *Antares* was reclassified in 1940 as a "general stores issue" ship. On the morning of the attack *Antares* was returning from a trip to Canton Island (halfway between Hawaii and Fiji) with a barge in tow and expecting to transfer it to a tug before proceeding into Pearl Harbor. *Antares* sighted a suspicious object 1500 yards from its starboard quarter and it reported it the destroyer *Ward* that was patrolling nearby. *Ward* sank the target, a Japanese *Ko-hyoteki*-class two-man midget submarine in what were the first American shots of the war. *Antares* reported being strafed by enemy planes at 0800. The ship zigzagged in restricted waters beyond the entrance to Pearl Harbor until granted permission at 1054 to enter Honolulu harbor and berth at 5-A.

Arare

The Japanese *Asashio*-class destroyer *Arare* ("Hailstone") was commissioned in April 1939. *Arare* served as part of Vice Admiral Nagumo's Carrier Strike Force accompanying it and guarding the fleet tankers. *Arare* was sunk in July 1942 by a torpedo from the submarine USS *Growler* 7 miles east of Kiska Harbor, Alaska.

Argonne (AG-31)

The miscellaneous auxiliary ship USS *Argonne* was flagship for Rear Admiral William L. Calhoun, Commander, Base Force, Pacific Fleet. It was berthed in the first repair slip at the north end of 1010 dock, with the minesweeper *Tern* alongside. In response to the attack, *Argonne* commenced fire from its antiaircraft battery of 3-inch guns and .50-caliber machine guns at 0758 and claimed shooting down one enemy plane as it flew over 1010 dock toward Ford Island. On the evening of December 7, one sailor was wounded and one killed by a .50-calber bullet fired from the direction of Ford Island where six aircraft from the *Enterprise* were attempting to land at the Naval Air Station and were mistaken for Japanese aircraft. *Argonne* left Pearl Harbor in April 1942 and served in the western Pacific for the remainder of the war. *Argonne* was originally assigned to the

U.S. Army Transport Service in early 1921 and subsequently commissioned by the U.S. Navy later in the year.

Arizona (BB-39)

The battleship USS *Arizona* was moored in mooring quays F-7 of Battleship Row forward of the *Nevada* and aft of the *Tennessee.* It was sunk and was a total loss. Alongside *Arizona* as of December 6, was the repair ship *Vestal* that was assisting with minor repairs. *Arizona* was a *Pennsylvania*-class battleship commissioned in October 1916. On December 7, the ship's air raid alarm sounded about 0755 sending the crew to general quarters shortly thereafter. Shortly after 0800 during the First Wave attack, 10 "Kate" torpedo bombers (5 from *Kaga* and 5 from *Hiryū*) attacked the ship from about 9,800 feet with 16.1-inch naval armor-piercing shells that had been modified and reshaped into 1757-lb aerial bombs. *Kaga*'s aircraft bombed the battleship from amidships to stern and *Hiryū*'s hit forward and the bow. There were 4 hits and 3 near misses with one of the misses causing observers to think a torpedo had hit the ship though no evidence has been found of such. The last bomb hit the ship at 0806 near Turret #2 on the starboard side igniting a fire and detonating the small black powder magazine between Turret #1 and #2 used for the catapults and about 7 seconds later the forward magazine with 500 tons of explosives in the powder magazine exploded destroying the forward part of the ship raining debris on Ford Island and creating intense fires that burned for 2 days. The explosion killed 1,177 of the 1,512 officers, sailors, and

Marines on board at the time comprising more than half of the lives lost during the attack and the ship sank in 9 minutes. The ship's Commanding Officer, Captain Franklin Van Valkenburg posthumously received the Medal of Honor for his efforts to fight for the ship. *Arizona* was placed "in ordinary" at Pearl Harbor on December 29, 1941, was struck from the Naval Vessel Register on December 1, 1942. Her wreck was cut down so that very little of the superstructure lay above water. The *Arizona* had 1.4 million gallons of fuel onboard when it sank, and about half a million gallons remain. About a quart and a half rises to the surface each day. Pearl Harbor survivors call the seepage "black tears."

Astoria (CL/CA-34)

The *New Orleans*-class heavy cruiser USS *Astoria* was en route to Midway Island 700 miles west of Hawaii with Task Force 12 with *Lexington, Chicago, Portland,* and 5 destroyers. After the attack *Astoria* searched for enemy ships and returned to Pearl Harbor on December 13. Originally commissioned in 1934 as the first in a class of cruisers but received a hull number higher than *New Orleans* due to being launched second in December 1933 and commissioned in April 1934. *Astoria* participated in the Battle of the Coral Sea and was sunk during the Battle of Savo Island, August 1942.

Avocet (AVP-4)

The USS *Avocet* was a seaplane tender moored at berth F-1, Naval Air Station Dock. It was undamaged in the attack.

Originally commissioned in 1918 as a *Lapwing*-class minesweeper, *Avocet* was recommissioned as a small seaplane tender in 1925. On December 7, security watches aboard *Avocet* reported seeing Japanese planes bombing seaplane hangars on Ford Island and sounded general quarters. A shot from *Avocet*'s 3-inch gun scored a direct hit on a Nakajima B5N2 "Kate" carrier attack bomber from the Japanese carrier *Kaga.* The bomber had just scored a torpedo hit on the battleship *California.* After being hit by fire from *Avocet*, the "Kate" crashed on the grounds of the naval hospital. At 1115 *Avocet* helped fight fires on the *California* and then was ordered to assist in the beaching and fighting fires of the battleship *Nevada,* doing so for two hours before successfully extinguishing them.

Aylwin (DD-355)

The destroyer USS *Aylwin* was berthed at buoy X-18 with *Dale* to port, followed by *Farragut* and *Monaghan,* and received minor damage to its propeller. The *Farragut*-class destroyer was commissioned in March 1935. At the time of the attack one small boiler was on line and half the crew was ashore on leave and liberty. By 0858 two boilers were operational and the ship headed for the channel and open sea with the crew under the direction of four ensigns, the senior one being Ensign Stanley B. Caplan. Machine gunners from the crew claimed to have shot down three enemy aircraft. Late on December 8, *Aylwin* returned to Pearl Harbor following the *Enterprise* task force.

* * *

This Japanese photo, captured later in the war, shows Battleship Row under attack by Japanese aircraft. Torpedo tracks head for USS *West Virginia* (BB-48) and USS *Oklahoma* (BB-37).

(National Archives photo)

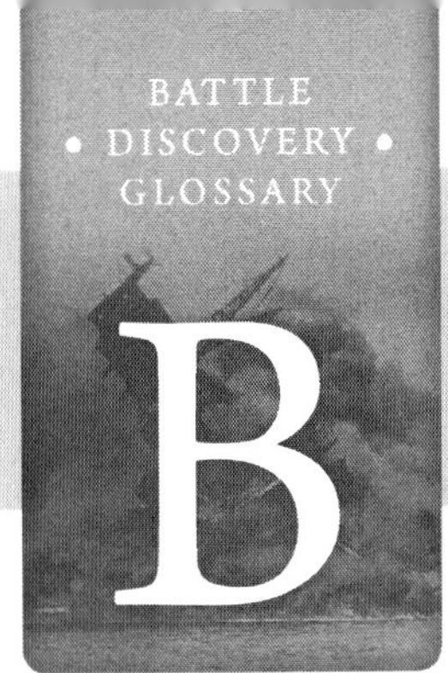

Bagley (DD-386)

The destroyer USS *Bagley* was at berth B-22, Navy Yard Pearl Harbor undergoing minor repairs. *Bagley* received minor damage from nearby explosions. Crew of *Bagley* fired .50-caliber guns at incoming Nakajima B5N "Kate" torpedo bombers during the First Wave and Aichi D3a "Val" dive-bombers during the Second Wave. *Bagley*'s battle report claimed to have shot down "five torpedo planes, one dive bomber and high altitude bomber" and claimed to be the "first ship to open fire on the enemy" firing at the third torpedo plane. At 0940 *Bagley* got underway and headed for the channel and the open sea under the temporary command of Lieutenant Philip W. Cann. The first in its class, it was commissioned in June 1937.

Barber's Point

As a military facility (naval air station), Barber's Point was not established until April 1942 (construction had commenced in November 1941). On December 8, there was an instance of mistaken identity and 4 fishing sampans were strafed by several Army P-40s killing 6 fishermen and wounding 7. In 1933 a lighthouse was constructed that served as a key navigational aid and still stands.

Battleship Row

Battleship Row was the name for the group of mooring quays on the east side of Ford Island where the battleships tied up. At the time of the attack battleships present were *Nevada, Arizona* (with repair ship *Vestal* moored alongside), *Tennessee, West Virginia, Maryland, Oklahoma, Neosho,* (oiler) and *California.* Nearby in dry dock No. 1 was *Pennsylvania.* Battleship Row was the primary target of the attack. Japanese operational planning priorities were to strike battleships and aircraft carriers. Japanese intelligence permitted the Japanese to know where individual battleships were likely to be moored and listed them in order of priority from 1 to 8. The Nakajima B5N2 "Kate" bombers were to attack the first four battleships and then strike the carriers if they were in port. If they were absent, the "Kates" were to attack battleships 5–8. The Aichi D3A/3A1 "Val" aircraft were to attack the carriers and if absent, then the cruisers. Outboard ships were attacked by torpedo planes and inboard ships were attacked by horizontal bombers.

Bellows Field

Bellows Field was created in 1917 as Waimanalo Military Reservation. Located in the southeast of Oahu, the airfield had its name changed to Bellows Field in 1933 and became a permanent military post in July 1941. It was one of

6 military airfields targeted (Hickam Field, Wheeler Field, Ford Island, Kanoehe Naval Air Station, Ewa Marine Corps Station, Bellows Field) but considered a secondary target by the Japanese. It was the base of the 86th Observation Squadron and 44th Pursuit Squadron On December 7, the airfield was a small installation but strafed by both waves of aircraft (but only 1 during the First Wave). Three P-40s tried to take off but one had its pilot killed as he was climbing into his aircraft, a second was shot down shortly after takeoff, and a third was shot down and crashed into the sea. A B-17 that landed was also strafed 15 minutes after arriving from California. From Belllows, 5 people were killed and 9 injured or wounded and 4 of 21 aircraft were destroyed. A Japanese 2-man midget submarine HA-19, commanded by Ensign Kazuo Sakamaki, grounded on the coral reef off Bellows Field. Sakamaki who swam ashore on December 8, was captured and became the first Japanese prisoner of war but Chief Warrant Officer Kiyoshi Inagaki, his crewmember, drowned.

Bennion, Mervyn S. (1887–1941)

Captain Mervyn S. Bennion was the Commanding Officer of the battleship *West Virginia* (BB-48). He was struck by shrapnel while on the ship's bridge. Messman Third Class Doris "Dorie" Miller and other crewmembers tried to move him to a first aid location but Captain Bennion refused to leave his post and died while still commanding the crew. He posthumously received the Medal of Honor.

Blue (DD-387)

The destroyer USS *Blue* was at berth X-7 and was undamaged in the attack. *Blue* was a *Bagley*-class destroyer commissioned in August 1937. *Blue* got underway during the attack with only four officers aboard (all Ensigns). The ship was sunk during the Battle of Guadalcanal in August 1942, being scuttled after taking a torpedo from the Japanese destroyer *Kawakaze.*

Bobolink (AM-20)

The USS *Bobolink* was a minesweeper moored in a nest at the westerly end of the Coal Docks with *Vireo* and *Turkey* inboard, and *Rail* outboard. It was undamaged in the attack. The ship fired upon Japanese aircraft and *Bobolink*'s after action report said that one Japanese aircraft was shot down as a result of firing coming from the minesweepers but no further specific ship confirmation could be given. *Boblink* was a *Lapwing*-class minesweeper commissioned in February 1919.

Boeing B-17

The Boeing B-17 "Flying Fortress" was a four-engine heavy bomber designed for the United States Army Air Corps in the 1930s. It had four 1,200 horsepower Wright R-1820–65 engines and was armed with seven .30-caliber machine guns (the B-17C had six .50-caliber machine guns and one .30-caliber, and the B17E had eight .50-caliber and one .30-caliber gun). On 07 December there were 12 Flying Fortresses at Hickam Field and group of 12 Flying Fortresses of the 38th (four B-17C) and 88th (eight B-17E) Reconnaissance Squadrons, were approaching

Hawaii after a 14-hour flight from Hamilton Field, California. They were en route to reinforce the Philippines and under the command of Major Truman Landon. The attack was in progress as the B-17s arrived and they were attacked by the Japanese and also mistakenly fired upon by Americans. The planes had been lightened for the long trip and were carrying no ammunition. The arriving B-17s were able to land at Hickam and Bellows Fields (and one on a golf course) but were heavily damaged and one crewman was killed. The attack on the B-17s lasted 10 minutes. U.S. Army radar at Opana and Kaswa sites briefly detected inbound aircraft at 0645 and 0702 and reported it but the planes mistakenly were assumed to be the B-17s when in fact, they were Japanese aircraft.

Boeing P-26

The Boeing P-26 "Peashooter" was designed in 1932 as the Army Air Corps' first all-metal fighter. It had an open cockpit and fixed landing gear but was obsolete by 1941. There were 14 on Oahu and all were damaged in the attack.

***Boggs* (DD-136/DMS-3)**

The USS *Boggs* was a *Wickes*-class destroyer commissioned in 1918 and reclassified in 1940 as a destroyer-minesweeper. At the time of the attack *Boggs* was at sea but returned to Pearl Harbor later in the day to sweep the approaches and anchorage for mines.

Bolo

See Douglas B-18.

Breese (DM-18)

The high-speed minelayer (converted Destroyer) USS *Breese* was moored in berth D-3, Middle Loch, in nest with other division minelayers. The order of the ships from starboard was *Ramsay*, *Breese*, *Montgomery*, and *Gamble. Breese* was undamaged. *Breese* was a *Wickes*-class destroyer commissioned as DD-122 in 1919 and reclassified as a light minelayer, DM-18, in January 1931. On 07 December, *Breese* began firing machine guns at enemy aircraft 0757 and is credited with several hits and also damaging one midget submarine.

A U.S. Army 38th Reconnaissance Squadron Boeing B-17E "Flying Fortress" (s/n 41-2408) that arrived over Oahu from California (USA) in the middle of the Japanese air raid with two Japanese Navy Aichi D3A1 Type 99 ("Val") carrier bombers flying nearby. When the photo was taken the plane was near Ewa Mooring Mast Field.

(Photograph SC 127014 Army Signal Corps Collection, National Archives)

* * *

USS *California,* afire and listing from two torpedo hits, settles to the harbor bottom. The guns from her No. 1 turret have been elevated through her awning.

(U.S. Navy History and Heritage Command photo)

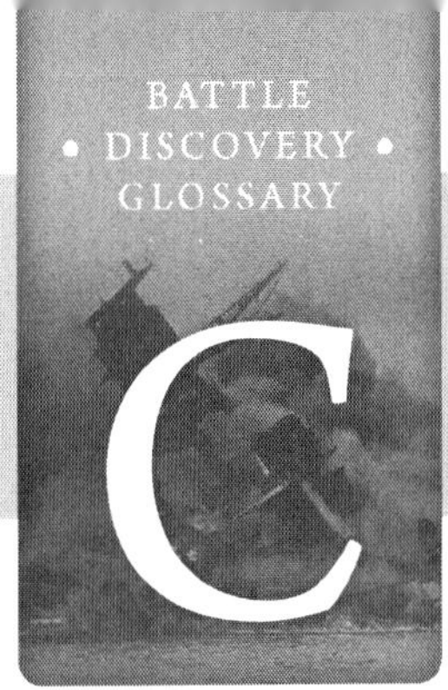

Cachalot (SS-170)

The submarine USS *Cachalot* was moored at berth B-1, Navy Yard, undergoing scheduled overhaul and was undamaged in the attack. *Cachalot* was the lead ship in the class and commissioned in December 1933 and served in the Pacific throughout 1942 as well as in the Bering Sea in support of the Aleutian Islands Campaign. In 1943, *Cachalot* became a training ship at the submarine school in New London, Connecticut.

Calhoun, William L. (1884–1963)

Rear Admiral (later Admiral) William L. Calhoun was serving as Commander, Base Force, Pacific Fleet. His flagship was USS *Argonne* (AG-31).

California (BB-44)

The battleship USS *California* was moored starboard side at mooring quay F-3. It was sunk but refloated and rebuilt by January 1944. It was the southernmost battleship on Battleship Row. *California* was preparing for an inspection on Monday morning, December 8, and the preparations left the watertight integrity compromised. This in turn, caused severe flooding when hit by bombs and a torpedo. Machine guns aboard commenced firing at 0803 and the first of 2 torpedoes hit at 0805 with the second following moments later. At 0845 a 551-lb bomb hit the starboard upper deck, passed through the main deck, and exploded on the armored second deck. This set off anti-aircraft ammunition and killed about 50 men. There were near-miss bombs and the explosion of 1 ruptured the bow plates. Smoke from fires caused evacuation of the forward engine room and the cessation of pumping effort to keep the ship afloat. After 3 days of flooding, *California* settled in the mud with only the superstructure appearing above water. There were 100 crewmembers killed and 62 wounded. By March 1942 the ship was refloated and in dry dock for repairs in Pearl Harbor before sailing to Puget Sound Navy Yard for major reconstruction and later serving in the Pacific in 1944 and 1945. *California* was a *Tennessee*-class battleship commissioned in 1921. It was capable of 21 knots and had 12 14-inch guns. *California* served as the flagship of the United States Battle Force and then as flagship of the United States Pacific Fleet when the Navy reorganized the structure in early 1941.

Case (DD-370)

The destroyer USS *Case* was moored starboard side of *Whitney* at berth X-8 undergoing regular scheduled overhaul. It was nested with *Conyngham*, *Reid*, *Tucker*, *Case* and *Selfridge* moored alongside to port and undamaged. *Case* was a *Mahan*-class destroyer commissioned in September 1936.

Casualties

The specific numbers was initially difficult to determine. The attack killed 2,390 U.S. personnel, including 49 civilians and wounded 1,178 servicemembers and 38 civilians. Other records place the number at 2,340 killed and 48 civilians with 1,143 wounded and 35 civilians. Japanese losses were 55 airmen and 9 midget submariners killed and 1 taken as a prisoner of war. Of the U.S casualties, approximately 1,177 were aboard the USS *Arizona.*

Cassin (DD-371)

The USS *Cassin* was a destroyer in dry dock with *Downes* and forward of *Pennsylvania. Cassin* was hit by at least one bomb It was burned and heavily damaged. Initially considered lost, *Cassin* was rebuilt and returned to service in February 1944. *Cassin* and *Downes* received similar damage. Bombs punctured their hulls releasing fuel oil that ignited. They were further damaged by exploding ammunition and the detonation of one of *Downes'* torpedoes. *Cassin* was a *Mahan*-class destroyer commissioned in August 1936. The hull was damaged beyond repair but other aspects of the ship were salvaged and sent to Mare Island Navy Yard where a new ship was built around the salvaged material and recommissioned with the same name and hull number in November 1943.

Castor (AKS-1)

The stores issue ship USS *Castor* was berthed at Merry Point berth M-1, near *Sumner* and was undamaged. Earlier in 1941,

Castor had carried U.S. Marine reinforcements to Wake Island and Johnston Island and 3 days before the attack had arrived in Pearl Harbor from San Francisco carrying explosives. Repeatedly strafed during the attack and returning fire with its .30-caliber machine guns, *Castor*'s crew had no loss of life or injuries. *Castor* was first of its class and commissioned in March 1941.

"Catalina"

See Consolidated PBY-5A.

Chandler (DD-206/DMS-9)

The USS *Chandler* was destroyer-minesweeper. *Chandler* was a *Clemson*-class destroyer commissioned in September 1919 but reclassified as a high-speed minesweeper in 1940. Homeported at Pearl Harbor, *Chandler* was at sea when the attack occurred but returned 2 days later.

Chew (DD-106)

The destroyer USS *Chew* was berthed at X-5 to with *Allen* and the decommissioned *Baltimore* that was being used for storage. *Chew* was undamaged in the attack. *Chew* opened fire on Japanese planes with its 3-inch .23-caliber gun at 0803 and its two .50-caliber machine guns at 0811 and kept firing until 0934 claiming 1 direct hit of a plane from the 3-inch gun. Two sailors were killed while engaged in rescue work and fighting fires on *Pennsylvania*. *Chew* got underway, patrolled southwest of the port entrance, and dropped 28 depth charges claiming the sinking of 2 submarines. Subsequent lack of evidence left the claim unsubstantiated. A *Wickes*-class destroyer commissioned in December 1918, *Chew* was placed out of commission in 1922 and recommissioned in October 1945.

Chicago (CA-29)

The USS *Chicago* was a *Northampton*-class commissioned in March 1931. Homeported at Pearl Harbor, *Chicago* was at sea with Task Force 12 on the day of the attack and returned on December 12 before resuming patrolling operations.

Chikuma

The *Chikuma* was a Japanese heavy cruiser named for the Chikuma River. It was the second and final ship in the *Tone*-class and was commissioned in May 1939. *Chikuma* was designed for long-range scouting and had the capacity for 6 seaplanes for reconnaissance. Along with sister ship *Tone*, the mission on December 7 was to provide weather reconnaissance and picket patrol and launched 1 Aichi 13A1 Type 0 "Jake" floatplane and 1 Nakajima E8N Type 95 "Dave" floatplane (*Tone* did the same, *Hiei* and *Kirishima* also launched floatplanes for patrol). One patrol plane was sent to Pearl Harbor and one to the fleet mooring at Lahaina Roads, Maui. *Chikuma* was sunk during the October 1944 Battle of Leyte Gulf.

"Climb Mount Niitaka"

"Climb Mount Niitaka" was the translation of *Niitaka yama nobore* and was the wording in the Japanese operational naval message sent on December 2 via J-25 code by Admiral Isoroku Yamamoto to the Pearl Harbor Strike Force under the command of Vice-Admiral Chuichi Nagumo indicating that the attack was to proceed as planned. It was sent after a final decision for war had been made in Tokyo.

Coal Dock
The coal dock was located at the end of South Avenue near Dry Dock No. 4. It was the first official Navy installation in Hawaii and was a fueling station for ships powered by coal. By the time of the attack, ships were diesel fuelled rather than coal fuelled. During the attack it was the site of the nesting of minesweepers *Bobolink*, *Rail*, *Turkey*, and *Vireo.*

Coast Guard
See U.S. Coast Guard.

***Cockatoo* (AMc-8)**
The USS *Cockatoo* was a coastal minesweeper and was undamaged in the attack. Commissioned in April 1941, *Cockatoo* operated in Hawaiian waters throughout the war.

***Condor* (AMc-14)**
The coastal minesweeper USS *Condor* returned to harbor from sweeping at 0525 and was undamaged in the attack. *Condor* was constructed as the wooden-hulled purse seiner *New Example* but acquired by the Navy in 1941 and converted to a coastal minesweeper and placed in service in April 1941.

On December 7, *Condor* made 0350 first contact with the Japanese and reported sighting a periscope to the USS *Ward* by visual signals at 0357 whereupon *Ward* began searching for the submarine. *Condor* operated in Hawaiian waters throughout the war.

Consolidated PBY-5A

Also known as the Canso, the Consolidated PBY-5A "Catalina," was one of the most widely used seaplanes of the war and was used in anti-submarine warfare, patrol bombing, search and rescue, convoy escorts, and cargo transport. PB stood for Patrol Bomber and Y was the company designation of Consolidated Aircraft. There were 39 based at Kaneohe Bay Naval Air Station at the time of the attack on Pearl Harbor and 23 with other patrol squadrons such as 12 with Patrol Squadron 22 Naval Air Station Pearl Harbor at Ford Island. Of the 61 all but 11 were destroyed or damaged. At 0700 a patrolling Catalina attacked a miniature submarine with depth charges.

Conyngham (DD-371)

The USS *Conyngham* was a destroyer moored starboard side to *Whitney* at berth X-8. *Reid, Tucker, Case* and *Selfridge* were nested outboard. Undamaged. *Conyngham* was a *Mahan*-class destroyer commissioned in November 1936. As part of the nest of destroyers, *Conyngham* opened fired on attacking aircraft of which several were downed. *Conyngham* in the Pacific throughout the war and used in 1946 Atomic Bomb tests and destroyed by sinking in 1948.

Crossbill (AMc-9)

The coastal minesweeper USS *Crossbill* returned to harbor from sweeping 0525 and was undamaged in the attack. Built in 1937 as *North Star,* the ship was acquired by the Navy in 1940 and commissioned as *Crossbill* in March 1941.

Cummings (DD-365)

The destroyer USS *Cummings* was nested at berth B-15 and the order of the ships there from the pier outboard was *Tracy*, *Preble*, and *Cummings.* Attacked by "Val" bombers at 0910 receiving minor damage from bomb fragments, *Cummings was* underway quickly but had 3 of the crew wounded. A *Mahan*-class destroyer, *Cummings* was commissioned in November 1936.

Curtiss (AV-22)

The USS *Curtiss* was a seaplane tender moored in berth X-22 across the channel from the *Utah.* It was hit by one crashed Val dive bomber flown by Lieutenant Mamoru Suzuki flying from *Akagi* at 0905 and one bomb at 0912. A second aircraft also crashed into it hitting the fantail. In spite of fires and damage, *Curtiss* continued firing throughout the attack and claimed 2 downed aircraft. Severely damaged, *Curtiss* returned to service January 1942. The first of its class, *Curtiss* was commissioned in November 1940.

Curtiss P-36

The Curtiss P-36 "Hawk" was originally created as the Curtiss Model 75A. It was a fighter aircraft (called pursuit aircraft during the war) flown by the U.S. Army Air Corps.

Curtiss P-40C

The Curtiss "Warhawk" was a fighter aircraft (called pursuit aircraft during the war) flown by the U.S. Army Air Corps and was a further development of the P-36. Two P-40Bs got airborne during the attack. Flown by Army 2nd Lieutenants George Welch and Kenneth Taylor from auxiliary Haleiwa Field where 18 P-40Bs were located, Taylor shot down 2 dive bombers and Welch downed 2 "Vals" and 1 Zero. Warhawks were the most numerous U.S. aircraft on Oahu.

Curtiss SOC

The Curtiss SOC "Seagull" was a single engine scout-observation biplane/floatplane that served on battleships and cruisers and was catapult launched. There were several on Ford Island at the time of the attack.

* * *

04-08

Moored as before. 0758 Waves of torpedo planes, level bombers, and dive bombers marked with Japanese insigna attacked Pearl Harbor; Sounded general quarters set condition afirm lit off boilers #1 and #2 and #4. Breaking out ammunition.

F.M. RADEL
Ensign, U.S. Navy

08-12

Moored as before. 0810 Opened fire on planes with machine guns followed by main battery. 0815 One enemy plane believed shot down by machine gun fire from USS DALE. 0825 Boilers #1, #2 and #4 cut in on main line. 0836 Underway on various courses and at various speeds proceeding out of Pearl Harbor. Ensign F.M. RADEL, U.S.N. Commanding Officer, following named Officers and men absent:- Lt.Comdr. A.L.Rorschach, U.S.N. Lt. R.L. Moore, Jr. U.S.N. Ensign K.G. Robinson, U.S.N. Ensign D.J. Vellis U.S.N. Ensign L.C. Huntley, U.S.N.R. Ensign M.E. Callahan U.S.N.R. EDWARDS, G.L. CMM U.S.N. WARREN, R.H. F.C.1c U.S.N. COULSON, S. E.M. 2c, U.S.N. SMITH, J.V. Sea 1c, U.S.N. FALCONER, D.D. Y1c, USS.N. NEHRING, R.A. F.C. 3c, U.S.N. GAMBILL, M. M.M.1c, U.S.N. ENGLISH, J.P. M.M. 1c, U.S.N. JENNINGS, A.V. F.2c, U.S.N. 0844 Stopped while USS MONAGHAN dropped two depth charges on what was thought to be and enemy submarine near USS CURTISS. 0848 Changed speed to 25 knots proceeding out of channel. 0907 Passed Pearl Harbor entrance buoy #1 passed from Inland to International waters. 0909 Established off shore patrol in sector #1 on various courses and at various speeds maneuvering to avoid strafing and bombing attacks. 0911 Shot down enemy dive bomber with .50 Caliber machine gun fire. 0959 Investigated small boat carrying small white flag with several Oriental passengers. 1114 Joined up with USS WORDEN (CDS-1) on course 340°T, 328°psc, speed 11 knots. 1149 Formed column, order of ships in column WORDEN, AYLWIN, DALE and FARRAGUT: on course 271°T, 260°psc, speed 25 knots.

F.M. RADEL
Ensign, U.S. Navy

The deck log of the USS *Dale* for December 7, 1941

(Personnel, RG 24 Records of the Bureau of Naval Personnel)

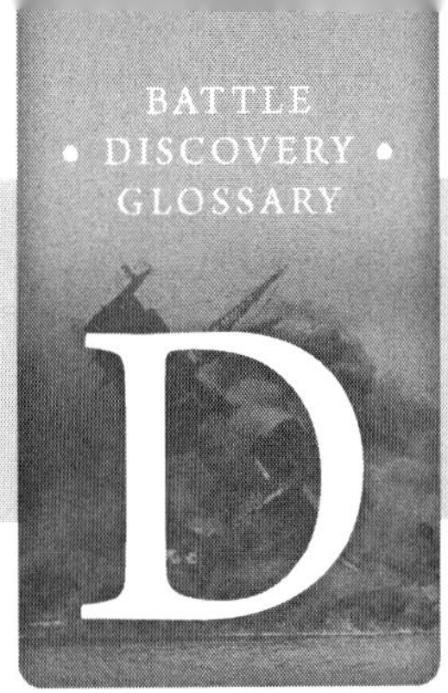

Dale (DD-353)

The USS *Dale* was a destroyer moored in the East Loch at X-14 with *Alwin, Farragut,* and *Monaghan. Dale* was undamaged and got underway about 0837 under command of the Command Duty Officer, an Ensign. *Dale* returned fire throughout the attack with no casualties. As *Dale* cleared the harbor entrance she came under intense bombing and fire by the Japanese in unsuccessful attempts to sink her and block the channel. At least one aircraft was downed by *Dale.* A *Farragut*-class destroyer commissioned in 1935. *Dale* served throughout the Pacific and in the Aleutians Campaign during the war.

Detroit (CL-8)

The USS *Detroit* was a light cruiser moored at berth F-13 aft of *Raliegh* and was undamaged. The ship claimed 2 Japanese aircraft brought down by joint anti-aircraft fire with *Curtiss. Detroit* was an *Omaha*-class light cruiser commissioned in July 1923 and during the war served in the South Pacific and Aleutians.

Dewey (DD-349)

The destroyer USS *Dewey* was moored berth X-2 with *Phelps*, *Macdonough*, *Worden*, *Hull* and *Dobbin* and undamaged. At the time of the attack *Dewey* was undergoing tender repairs. *Dewey* returned anti-aircraft fire and got underway in the afternoon following the attack. A *Farragut*-class destroyer commissioned in 1934 and served throughout the Pacific during the war.

Dobbin (AD-3)

The destroyer tender USS *Dobbin* was at berth X-2, nested with *Hull*, *Dewey*, *Worden*, *Macdonough*, and *Phelps* north of Ford Island; minor damage from bomb burst. *Dobbin* engaged Japanese with anti-aircraft fire along with other ships nested together and had 2 fatalities. *Dobbin* served in Hawaiian area and Australia for remainder of the war. *Dobbin* was commissioned in July 1924.

Dolphin (SS-169)

The submarine USS *Dolphin* was moored port side to, Pier 4, in berth S-8, at the Submarine Base and was undamaged. *Dolphin* was 1 of 9 "V-boat" designed submarines. It was commissioned June 1937 and served in the Pacific throughout the war.

Douglas A-20

The Douglas A-20 "Havoc" was built by Douglas Aircraft with a company designation of DB-7. It was an American attack, light bomber.

Douglas B-18

The Douglas B-18 "Bolo" was a medium bomber of the United States Army Air Corps. On the day of the attack there were 33 assigned (21 in commission) to 18th Bombardment Wing at Hickam Field. After the attack there were 21 available (11 in commission).

Douglas SBD

The Douglas SBD "Dauntless" was a carrier-based scout plane and dive-bomber and was the U.S. Navy's primary aircraft. It was also used by the U.S. Marine Corps. The plane could carry a 1000-pound bomb under the fuselage and two 100-pound bombs beneath its wings. Most of the planes at Pearl Harbor were destroyed or damaged in the attack. SBDs from *Yorktown* were critical in the American victory on 4 June 1942 at the Battle of Midway.

Downes (DD-375)

The destroyer USS *Downes* was in Dry Dock No. 1 with *Cassin* and *Pennsylvania*; heavily damaged, initially considered lost, but rebuilt and recommissioned November 15, 1943. An incendiary bomb landed between *Cassin* and *Downes* creating fires fuelled by oil from a ruptured tank. *Downes* returned anti-aircraft fire the dry dock was flooded to assist in damage control but when fires on the rising water began to ignite ammunition and torpedoes onboard, both *Downes* and *Cassin* were ordered abandoned.

Downes was a *Mahan*-class destroyer commissioned in January 1937, decommissioned in June 1942, and recomissioned in November 1943 and served in the Pacific for the remainder of the war.

Dry Dock Number 1

Dry Dock Number 1 was part of the Pearl Harbor Naval Shipyard and 1 of 4 permanent dry docks. The dry dock was constructed and opened in 1919 after the crumbling and collapse of a previous one in 1913. It had *Pennsylvania, Cassin,* and *Downes* in it at the time of the attack.

USS *Dolphin*

(U.S. Navy photo, National Archives)

* * *

The burning wreckage of an U.S. Marine Corps Douglas SBD *Dauntless* dive bomber pictured at Ewa Mooring Mast Field (later Marine Corps Air Station (MCAS) Ewa, Hawaii) after the Japanese attack.

(U.S. Navy – U.S. Navy National Museum of Naval Aviation photo No. 1996.488.029.040)

BATTLE
• DISCOVERY •
GLOSSARY

E

East Loch
See Pearl Harbor.

Egusa, Takashige (1907–1944)
Lieutenant Commander Takashige Egusa was the Imperial Japanese Navy pilot who led the Second Wave of 81 Aichi D3A1 "Vals" in his unique flame-red aircraft.

***Elliot* (DD-146)**
The *Wickes*-class destroyer USS *Elliot* was originally commissioned in January 1919. *Elliot* was returning from Johnston Island with Task Force 3 at the time of the attack and immediately began anti-submarine operations.

Elliot, George Jr. (1918–2003)
George Elliot Jr. was a U.S. Army private and radar operator whose warnings of approaching aircraft along with those of Private Joseph Lockard went unheaded by inexperienced Navy Lieutenant Kermit Tyler and were dismissed as the incoming flight of American B-17s arriving from California.

Embargo

An embargo was part of the economic measures taken against Japan to attempt to stem Japanese militarism and expansion into China, President Franklin D. Roosevelt signed the Export Control Act on 02 July 1940 that allowed him to limit or prohibit export of essential defense materials. This was later expanded to an embargo of oil, scrap iron, and steel destined for Japan. In July1941, all Japanese assets in the United States were frozen, further restricting Japanese economic capabilities.

Enterprise (CV-6)

The *Yorktown*-class aircraft carrier USS *Enterprise* was commissioned in May 1938 as the sixth U.S. Navy aircraft carrier. *Enterprise* was at sea on the morning of the attack and returned in the evening for fuel and supplies before getting underway again. The Japanese had hoped find all 3 of the U.S. Pacific Fleet carriers (*Enterprise, Lexington, Saratoga*) in port but did not do so.

Ewa Mooring Mast Field

Ewa Field was a Marine Corps Air Station built in 1925 located 7 miles west of Pearl Harbor. On the day of the attack it was the first installation hit by the Japanese and all 48 aircraft based there were destroyed.

USS *Enterprise* in 1939. *Enterprise* was one of the "missing" carriers from Pearl Harbor that the Japanese hoped were in port.

* * *

Photograph taken from a Japanese plane during the torpedo attack on ships moored on both sides of Ford Island shortly after the beginning of the Pearl Harbor attack. Japanese writing in the lower right states that the photograph was reproduced by authorization of the Navy Ministry.

(Official U.S. Navy photograph NH 50930)

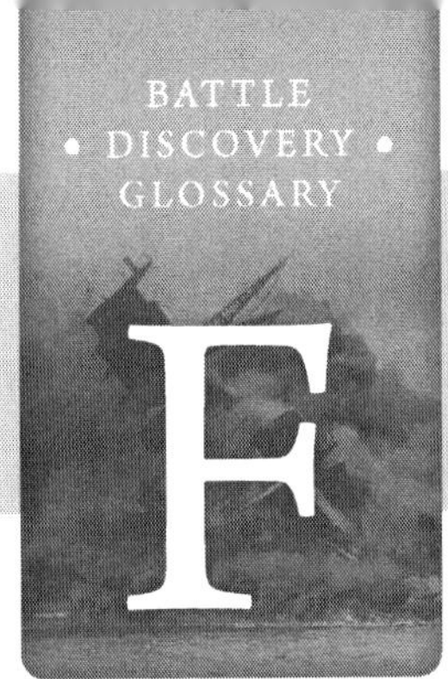

Farragut (DD-348)

The destroyer USS *Farragut* was berthed in nest in East Loch with *Aylwin, Dale,* and *Monaghan* and received minor damage from strafing. During the attack the ship got underway and went down the channel as it kept up anti-aircraft fire until it cleared the channel at 0927. *Farragut* was the lead ship in its class and was commissioned in June 1934 and served in the Pacific throughout the war.

Fifth Carrier Division (Japanese)

The Fifth Carrier Division was an aircraft carrier unit of the Imperial Japanese Navy. During the attack on Pearl Harbor it consisted of the carriers *Akagi* and *Kaga* and was commanded by Rear Admiral Hara Chuichi.

First Carrier Division (Japanese)

The First Carrier Division was an aircraft carrier unit of the Imperial Japanese Navy. During the attack on Pearl Harbor it consisted of the carriers *Shōkaku* and *Zuikaku* and was commanded by Vice Admiral Chuichi Nagamo

First Carrier Striking Force (Japanese)
The First Carrier Striking Force consisted of the IJN carriers employed on December 7: *Akagi, Kaga, Sōryū, Hiryū, Zuikaku, Shōkaku.*

First Submarine Group (Japanese)
The First Submarine group was comprised of *I-9, I-15, I-17,* and *I-25* and was commanded by Rear Admiral Tsutome Sato.

First Wave (Japanese)
The First Wave, also called First Attack Wave, was the first of two planned air attacks on U.S. forces at Pearl Harbor and on Oahu. The First Wave was comprised of 183 aircraft (originally 189, but 6 failed to launch) launched from 6 IJN carriers north of Oahu (*Akagi, Kaga, Sōryū, Hiryū, Shōkaku, Zuikaku*). Led by Commander Mitsuo Fuchida, there were 3 groups: the 1st Group targets were to be battleships and aircraft carriers, although no carriers were in port, and consisted of 49 Nakajima "Kate" bombers with armor-piercing bombs, and 40 "Kates" with Type 91 torpedoes; the 2nd Group targets were Ford Island and Wheeler Field and consisted of 51 Aichi D3A "Val" dive bombers; the 3rd Group targets were aircraft at Ford Island, Hickam Field, Wheeler Field, Barber's Point, and Kaneohe Naval Air Station and consisted of 43 Mitsubishi A6M "Zero" fighters. The aircraft struck at 0748 and ended at 0810. Nine of the aircraft were lost in the First Wave. In the First Wave the "Kates" attacked the ships and the "Vals" attacked the land targets. In the Second Wave these roles were reversed.

First Wave First Group (Japanese)

This Japanese attack group, often seen in historical records as "1st Group," consisted of 49 Nakajima "Kate" bombers with armor-piercing bombs, and 40 "Kates" with Type 91 torpedoes. Its targets were to be battleships and aircraft carriers, although no carriers were in port.

First Wave Second Group (Japanese)

This Japanese attack group, also listed sometimes as "2nd Group," consisted of 51 Aichi D3A Val dive bombers. Its targets were to be Ford Island and Wheeler Field.

First Wave Third Group (Japanese)

This Japanese attack group, also listed sometimes as "3rd Group," consisted of 43 Mitsubishi A6M Zero fighters. Its targets were to be aircraft at Ford Island, Hickam Field, Wheeler Field, Ewa Mooring Mast Field, and Kaneohe Naval Air Station.

***Flusser* (DD-368)**

The USS *Flusser* was a *Mahan*-class destroyer commissioned in October 1963. *Flusser* was at sea on training operations with *Lexington* at the time of the attack and returned to port on December 12 after searching for the retiring Japanese fleet.

"Flying Fortress"

See Boeing B-17.

Ford Island, Naval Air Station Pearl Harbor

The naval air station was a 441-acre site that was the epicenter of the attack. Originally a base for U.S. Army aviation (Luke Field), it was turned over to the Navy in 1939 as a location for battleships and submarines. It was the site of Battleship Row moorings and also headquarters of Patrol Wing 2. As a seaplane base it had 4 squadrons of PBY Catalina patrol bombers with an operational radius of 700 miles and other aircraft. Had the carriers been in port, they would have been moored at Ford Island. Because of communications confusion, Ford Island was attacked several minutes before the torpedo bombers struck the battleships. A bomb intended for the *California* hit Hangar 6 igniting it. Other bombs hit Hangar 38 and the dispensary courtyard. Thirty-three of the 70 planes on the island were destroyed. The name Ford Island derived from its ownership in the nineteenth century by physician Seth Porter Ford. In Hawaiian, Ford Island was known as *Poka 'Ailana* and also by its original native name *Moku'ume'ume* (Island of Attraction). Westerners had known it as Rabbit Island, Marín Island, and Little Goats Island.

Forgy, Howell M. (1908–1972)

Howell M. Forgy was a U.S. Navy chaplain (Lieutenant) assigned to *New Orleans*. As crewmembers of *New Orleans* fired 5-inch anti-aircraft shells at Japanese aircraft and struggled to manually pass ammunition and operate the gun, Forgy encouraged them with the words "praise the Lord and pass the ammunition." Reports of this spread and the words were put to music with the same title by Frank Loesser. By December 1942, the song was in the number 2 popularity position, just behind Bing Crosby's "White Christmas."

Fort Kamehameha

Fort Kamehameha was a U.S. Army installation originally established at Fort Upton in 1907 on Queen Emma Point on Oahu (on the eastern side of the harbor entrance). It was the home of the 5th Battalion 55th Coast Artillery with 155mm mobile guns and .30-caliber machine guns. One Japanese Mitsubishi A6M2 "Zero" from the carrier *Akagi* was shot down and crashed into the the side of Building 52, the ordnance machine killing the pilot and 4 men inside the building The pilot, who was killed, was NAP1/c Takeshi Hirano. Plane's tail code was "AI-154."

Fort Shafter

Dating from 1907, Fort Shafter was the oldest military base on Oahu and home of the Hawaiian Army Command that was comprised of the U.S. Army components in Hawaii and was commanded by Lieutenant General Walter C. Short.

Fuchida, Mitsuo (1902–1976)

Commander Mitsuo Fuchida was the air-strike leader and led the First Wave in a Nakajima B5N2 "Kate" from the *Akagi* piloted by Lieutenant Mitsuo Matsuzaki. He had gained combat experience in air operations over China in the 1930s and was considered one of Japan's best naval aviators. At 0749 Fuchida instructed his radio operator, Petty Officer 1st Class Norinobu Mizuki to send planes in his own formation the attack order "To, To, To," the first syllable of *totsugeki seyo* meaning "charge" or "strike." Four minutes later, at 0753, Fuchida ordered Mizuki to send the code words "Tora, tora, tora" back to the carrier *Akagi*, the flagship of 1st Air Fleet broadcasting that the Japanese had achieved surprise in the attack. Due to favorable atmospheric conditions, the transmission of the "Tora, tora, tora" code words from the moderately powered transmitter were heard over a ship's radio in Japan by Admiral Isoroku Yamamoto, Japan's wartime naval commander. As the first wave returned to the carriers, Fuchida remained over the target to assess damage and observe the second-wave attack. He returned to his carrier after the second wave had completed its mission. Fuchida was on board the Japanese carrier *Akagi* during the Battle of Midway. He was injured in the air attack against it and was saved from the sinking carrier. Upon returning to Japan, he was ordered to the Naval War College as an instructor and directed to prepare a highly secret report on the battle. He was promoted to captain and served as the fleet air staff officer at the Battle of the Philippine Sea in June 1944.

Fuel storage tanks

The fuel storage tanks containing 4.5 million gallons of fuel oil were not attacked. Partially this was because smoke from them would have prevented visibility of the main targets. Admiral Yamamoto's original plan was that a third attack wave would strike these facilities but Admiral Nagumo's decision not to risk the carriers or planes in a third wave attack left repair capabilities and fuel stores undamaged. Many have argued that had they been destroyed, the Pacific Fleet would have had to return to the west coast of the U.S. for homeporting and the ability to begin a counter-offensive would have been significantly delayed.

Aerial view the fuel storge tanks the the left of the submarine base, looking south on October 13, 1941.

(U.S. Navy photo 80-G-182880)

* * *

Minoru Genda

16 August 1904–15 August 1989

One of the planners of the attack

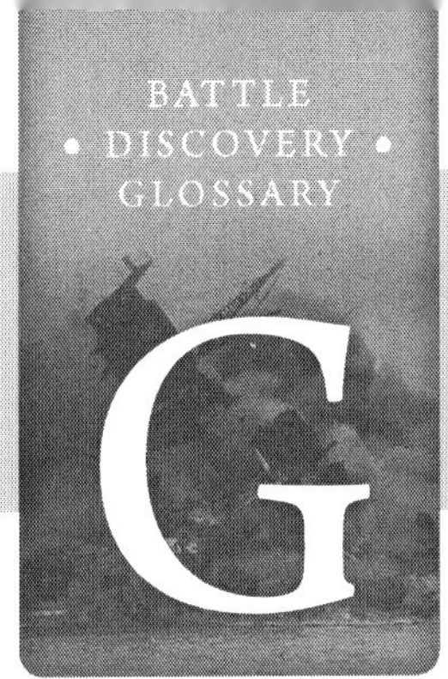

Gamble (DM-15)

The high-speed minelayer (converted destroyer) USS *Gamble* was moored in berth D-3, Middle Loch, in nest with division, order of ships from starboard *Ramsay*, *Breese*, *Montgomery*, and *Gamble* and was undamaged. *Gamble* was first commissioned in November 1918 as a *Wickes*-class destroyer. In May 1930 *Gamble* was reclassified as a minelayer. On the morning of the attack *Gamble* participated in anti-aircraft fire and *Gamble*'s after action report stated that one aircraft was believed to have been shot down by the ship's gunners.

Genda, Minoru (1904–1989)

Commander (later, Captain) Minoru Genda, was an IJN commander who was one of the planners of the attack. He was a well-known naval aviator in Japan and understood the potential of massed raids by aircraft from multiple carriers. This was contrary to the thought of most strategists who conceived of either single carriers launching aircraft for raids or air fleet aircraft being used as cover for bombers. Genda gained combat experience in 1937 in China and was a longtime advocate of air power.

Grebe (AM-43)

The minesweeper USS *Grebe* was at berth B-20, Navy Yard, alongside *Schley;* undamaged. *Grebe* was commissioned in May 1919. On the day of the attack *Grebe* was in yard availability and its 3-inch guns had been removed with the result that only rifles and pistols were available for use.

Grumman F4F

The Grumman F4F "Wildcat" was a monoplane that carried 4 Browning .50-caliber machine guns. There were 11 assigned to Marine Air Group 21 at Ewa Field and all were destroyed in the First Wave.

Grumman F4F "Wildcat" (post-1941 version)

(National Archives)

* * *

Ha-19 grounded in the surf on Oahu near Bellows Field after the attack on Pearl Harbor.

(U.S. Navy Military History Center. Photo # NH 91331)

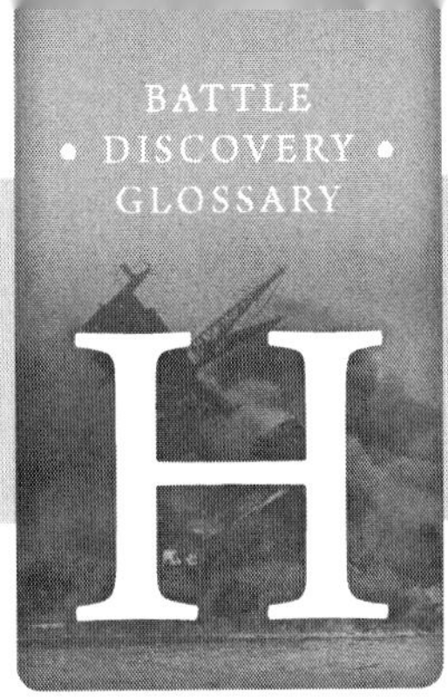

Ha-19

See Midget submarine.

Hachimaki

The *Hachimaki* is a headband that is worn by Japanese warriors as a sign of perseverance or courage. Usually made of red or white cloth, *Hachimaki* are decorated with encouraging words and phrases, and nearly all of them have a depiction of the rising sun in the front. Though often identified with the kamikaze pilots later in the war, they were worn during the attack on Pearl Harbor as can be seen in many of the photographs of the Japanese pilots preparing for the attack. Attack commander Mitsuo Fuchida was given a white one to wear by the senior maintenance crewman on the *Akagi*. Touched by the gesture, Fuchida tied it samurai-fashion around his helmet and wore it throughout the attack.

Haleiwa Field

Haleiwa Field was a U.S. Army Air Corps unpaved auxiliary airstrip to Wheeler Field and was originally used as an emergency runway. On December 7, it had a variety of aircraft temporarily assigned to it including 8 Curtiss P-40 "Warhawk" and 2 Curtiss P-36 "Mohawk" aircraft from the 47th Fighter Squadron. A total of nine Japanese aircraft were shot down by pilots from the Haleiwa field during the Pearl Harbor attack, especially notable were 4 by 2nd Lt. George S. Welch and 2nd Lt. Kenneth M. Taylor, who shot down 2. Both Welch and Taylor were flying the P-40. Second Lieutenant Harry W. Brown who was flying a P-36A also shot down 1 plane. The site of the Haleiwa Fighter Strip is located north of the intersection of Route 83 and Kahalewai Place, Haleiwa.

Hamakaze

The Japanese *Kagerō*-class destroyer *Hamakaze* ("Beach Wind"), was a commissioned in June 194 that was part of Division 17. It was sunk in April 1945 by aircraft from USS *Hornet* (CV-12) and USS *Cabot* (CVL-28).

Hasegawa, Kiichi (1894–1944)

Captain Kiichi Hasegawa was the captain of *Akagi* which was the flagship for Admiral Chuichi Nagumo during the attack. He was promoted to Rear Admiral and participated in many carrier battles until being killed in action in March 1944.

Havoc

See Douglas A-20.

Hawaiian Air Force

The Hawaiian Air Force was established in 1940 as a part of the 1939–1940 expansion program of the U. S. Army Air Corps and had headquarters at Fort Shafter. It consisted of the 18th Bombardment Wing at Hickam Field and the 14th Pursuit Wing at Wheeler Field. At the time of the attack the Hawaiian Air Force consisted of 754 officers and 6,706 enlisted men with 231 aircraft. None of the aircraft were loaded with bombs or ammunition prior to the attack due to concern of sabotage. In order to guard sabatoge, orders were issued orders pertaining to aircraft on the ground. This included tightly lining up and grouping aircraft, removing and storing bombs, and unloading guns and placing ammunition in hangars each night. The attack caused significant damage in which Hawaiian Air Force casualties were 163 killed, 43 missing, and 336 wounded, of which most were at Hickam Field. There were 64 aircraft destroyed and fewer than 79 left usable and only 39 combat worthy. In February 1942, the Hawaiian Air Force was re-designated 7th Air Force.

"Hawaii Operation"

"Hawaii Operation" was a Japanese term for the attack on Pearl Harbor. It was also called "Operation AI" by the Japanese Imperial General Headquarters and "Operation Z" in its planning phase.

Helm (DD-388)

The *Bagley*-class destroyer USS *Helm* was commissioned in October 1937. It was underway from berth X-7 just prior to attack, en route to degaussing buoys at West Loch; minor damage by two bomb near-misses. It was the only ship underway during the attack and is credited with downing 1 Japanese aircraft. At 0817 it left West Loch for the open sea through the Pearl Harbor Inlet. While doing so, a lookout spotted the midget submarine *No. 19* (also known as *Ha-19*) caught on a reef and attacked it. *No. 19* escaped, submerged, but caught again and was abandoned by its crew. One crewmember drowned and the second, Kazu Sakamaki, became the first Japanese prisoner of war for the Americans. *Helm* served throughout the Pacific during the war and was decommissioned in 1946.

Helena (CL-50)

The *St. Louis*-class light cruiser USS *Helena* was commissioned in September 1939. It was moored at 1010 Dock Navy Yard at berth B-2 with *Oglala* outside. By chance, it was moored in the berth normally assigned to battleship *Pennsylvania* and was thus a prime target. It was hit by one torpedo and seriously damaged; returned to service January 1942. It served throughout the Pacific and was sunk at the Battle of Kula Gulf on July 6, 1943.

Henley (DD-391)

The USS *Henley* was a *Bagley*-class destroyer commissioned in August 1937. At the beginning of the attack it was moored in

East Loch with *Patterson* and *Ralph Talbot* at berth X-11and received minor damage from strafing. It got underway, dropped depth charges on a sonar contact and is crediting with downing 1 Japanese aircraft and sharing credit for a second. *Henley* was sunk by a torpedo fired from Japanese submarine *Ro-108* on October 3, 1943.

Hiei

The *Hiei* was a Japanese *Kongo*-class battlecruiser commissioned in 1914 and reconstructed in 1937 as a battleship. It sailed as part of the attacking force protecting the 6 Japanese aircraft carriers. It participated in many actions in early 1942 and was sunk following the naval battle of Guadalcanal on November 14, 1942 after being struck by 4 torpedoes from aircraft of USS *Enterprise* (CV-6).

Hickam Field

Hickam Field was constructed by the Army Air Corps and activated in September 1939, the airfield was the principle army airfield in Hawaii and the only one large enough to accommodate B-17s. It was 1 of 6 airfields attacked and was a major target and attacked during both waves. During the attack it was bombed and strafed by the Japanese to prevent aircraft from engaging Japanese aircraft and following them as they returned to their carriers. The morning of the attack there were 12 B-17s scheduled to land at Hickam. Japanse bombers concentrated their attack on the airfield on hangars and barracks and Japanese fighters primarily attacked parked aircraft lined closely together to prevent sabotage. Hickam had casualties of 189 killed and 303 wounded.

Hirohito (1901–1989)

Referred to today primarily by his posthumous name, Emperor Shōwa, Hirohito was the 12th Emperor of Japan and ruled from 1929 until his death in 1989. In September 1940, Japan signed the Tripartite Pact with Germany and Italy in which they pledged to come to each other's aid if attacked by a country not already in the war. When plans were produced for the attack on Pearl Harbor, Hirohito consented in early November 1941 to the decision of the government that functioned under the Constitution of the Empire of Japan (known in formally as the Meiji Constitution) that was in force from November 1890 until May 1947 and mixed constitutional and absolute monarchy forms of government. The extent of Hirohito's involvement in war decisions as well as the extent of his control over the military during the Second World War remains controversial. He was not charged or tried as a war criminal after the war.

Hiryū

The Japanese aircraft carrier *Hiryū* ("Flying Dragon") was the flagship of the Second Carrier Division and was commanded by Captain Tomeo Kaku. Commissioned in 1939, it was the only ship of its class and was built on a modified *Sōryū* design. It was 1 of 6 Japanese carriers that participated in the attack (*Akagi, Kaga, Hiryū, Shōkaku, Sōryū, Zuikaku*), employing a force of 21 Mitsubishi A6M "Zero" fighters, 18 Aichi

D3A "Val" dive bombers, and 18 Nakajima B5N "Kate" torpedo bombers. *Hiryū* was damaged and subsequently scuttled during the Battle of Midway on June 5, 1942.

Hitokappu Bay

Also known as Tankan Bay, Hitokappu Bay is located on the island of Etorofu in the southern Kurile Islands of Japan. It was the assembly point for the Japanese Pearl Harbor strike force and was chosen because of its isolation. Oilers were brought to the bay to top off the strike force before it sailed for Pearl Harbor on November 26, 1941. The site had little further role in the war.

***Hoga* (YT-46/YTB-146/YTM-146)**

Hoga was a *Woban*-class district harbor tugboat named after the Sioux word for "fish. *Hoga* was placed into service with the U.S. Navy on May 22, 1941, and allocated to the 14th Naval District at the Naval Station in Pearl Harbor. *Hoga*, particularly distinguished herself through her crew's actions in helping beach the burning and sinking battleship USS *Nevada* (BB 36) at Hospital Point. The yard tug also fought fires on Battleship Row for 48 hours and rescued wounded sailors from the oily waters. For the remainder of World War II *Hoga* served in Pearl Harbor.

***Honolulu* (CL-48)**

The USS *Honolulu* was a *Brooklyn*-class light cruiser commissioned in June 1938 and moored at berth B-21, Navy Yard, with *St. Louis* outboard. *Honolulu* received light damage and remained in service throughout the war serving in the Pacific.

Hovey (DD-208/DMS-11)

The USS *Hovey* was a *Clemson*-class destroyer commissioned in September 1919 and converted and reclassified as a high-speed minesweeper in November 1940. At the time of the attack *Hovey* was engaged in gunnery practice 20 miles from Pearl Harbor. It was sunk in battle on January 7, 1945.

Hospital Point

This was the site of U.S. Naval Hospital Pearl Harbor. The hospital had a capacity of approximately 250 beds. The hospital was slightly damaged during the attack and a total of 546 battle casualties and 313 dead were brought to the hospital on December 7th. There were approximately 452 casualties were admitted to the hospital in less than three hours. There was no record kept of more than 200 men who received first aid for minor injuries and were returned to duty immediately without being admitted. The hospital census of patients at midnight, December 7, was 960. The USS *Nevada* grounded ¼ mile from Hospital Point at 1030 on the morning of the attack.

Hulbert (DD-342/AVD-6)

The USS *Hulbert* was commissioned as a *Clemson*-class destroyer in October 1920 and converted and reclassified as a seaplane tender destroyer (AVD) in August 1940. At the time of the attack, *Hulbert* was moored berth S-3 at the Submarine Base. Undamaged in the attack, *Hulbert* was credited with shooting down 1 torpedo plane, shared in bringing down a dive bomber, and damaged several other aircraft. After the attack the ship assisted in the rescue effort. The ship served in the Aleutians Campaign and was decommissioned in November 1945.

Hull (DD-350)

The USS *Hull* was a *Farragut*-class destroyer commissioned in January 1935. It was at berth X-2, nested with *Dobbins*, *Dewey*, *Worden*, *Macdonough*, and *Phelps* undergoing repairs and received minor damage from a bomb near-miss. Using anti-aircraft fire, *Hull* assisted in the downing of Japanese aircraft. *Hull* served throughout the Pacific but sank on December 18, 1944 in a typhoon with a loss of more than 200 crewmembers.

Hull, Cordell (1871–1955)

Cordell Hull was the U.S. Secretary of State who met with Japan's ambassador Admiral Kichisaburo Nomura and envoy Saburo Kurusa at 1420 Washington, D.C. time just after President Franklin D. Roosevelt telephoned Hull with news of the attack. Ambassador Noruma handed Hull a diplomatic message breaking diplomatic relations that Hull had already seen due to interception and translation by American intelligence. The meeting with Hull had been postponed from

1300 due to Japanese difficulties in receiving and translating the message and came too late as the attack had already occurred. The message had arrived in 14 parts and had to be decoded and translated. The original intent was that it would be delivered 30 minutes prior to the attack but its delay in translation cast Nomura into the unfortunate and unknowing role of messenger after the fact.

U.S. flag flies over Hickham Field after the attack

(National Archives)

* * *

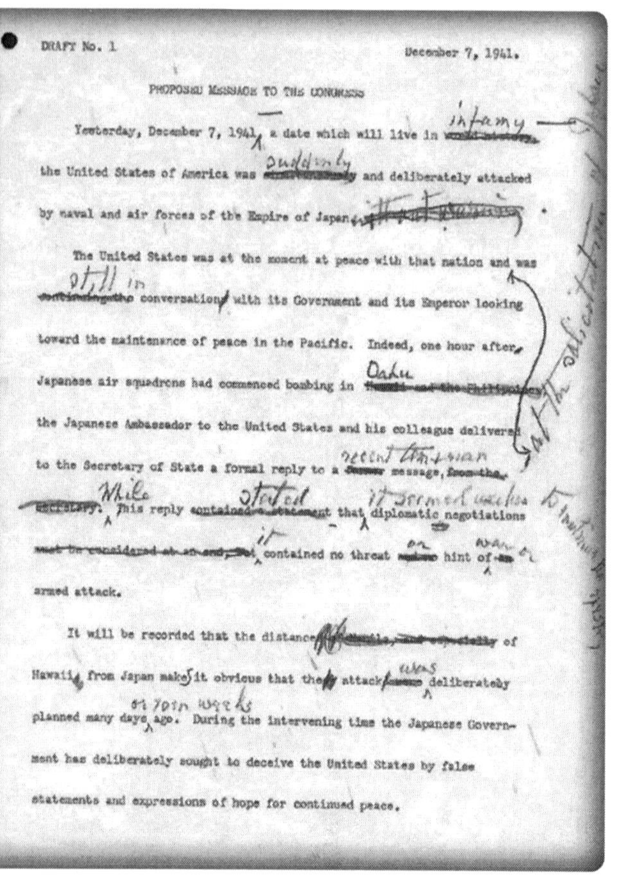

DRAFT No. 1 December 7, 1941.

PROPOSED MESSAGE TO THE CONGRESS

Yesterday, December 7, 1941, a date which will live in infamy the United States of America was suddenly and deliberately attacked by naval and air forces of the Empire of Japan.

The United States was at the moment at peace with that nation and was still in conversation with its Government and its Emperor looking toward the maintenance of peace in the Pacific. Indeed, one hour after Japanese air squadrons had commenced bombing in Oahu the Japanese Ambassador to the United States and his colleague delivered to the Secretary of State a formal reply to a recent American message. While this reply stated that it seemed useless to continue the existing diplomatic negotiations it contained no threat or hint of war or armed attack.

It will be recorded that the distance of Hawaii from Japan makes it obvious that the attack was deliberately planned many days or even weeks ago. During the intervening time the Japanese Government has deliberately sought to deceive the United States by false statements and expressions of hope for continued peace.

First draft of the "Infamy Speech" with hand corrections by President Roosevelt

(National Archives photo)

_I-16_

I-16 was the Japanese fleet submarine that carried *Ha A*, a Type-A midget submarine under Lieutenant Junior Grade Yokoyama Masaharu with PO2C Ueda Sadamu. It was the first of five midgets released at 0042 by the Special Attack Unit. *I-16* was sunk off the Solomon Islands in May 1944.

_I-18_

I-18 was the Japanese fleet submarine that carried *Ha E*, a Type-A midget submarine that was launched about 0215 under Lieutenant Junior Grade Furuno Shigemi and PO1C Yokoyama Shigenori. *I-16* served in the Pacific until February 1943 when contact was lost and it was presumed sunk in the Coral Sea after being depth charged by USS *Fletcher* (DD-445).

_I-20_

I-20 was the Japanese fleet submarine that carried *Ha D*, a Type-A midget submarine that was launched at 0257 under Ensign Hiroo Akira with PO2C Katayama Yoshio. *I-20* likely was sunk by USS *Ellet* (DD-398) off Espiritu Santo in September 1943.

I-21

I-21 was the Japanese fleet submarine that patrolled north of Oahu during the attack. It likely was torpedoed and sunk by TBF "Avengers" off Tarawa on 29 November 1943.

I-22

I-22 was the Japanese fleet submarine that carried *Ha B,* a Type-A midget submarine that was launched 9 miles from the harbor entrance at 0116 under Lieutenant Iwasa Naoji with PO1C Sasaki Naoyoshi. *I-22* likely was sunk by a PBY-5A "Catalina" flying boat, after delivering oxygen bottles and personnel to Henderson Field, Guadalcanal after the plane spotted and dropped 4 depth charges on an unidentified Japanese submarine.

I-24

I-24 was the Japanese fleet submarine that carried *Ha C, No. 19,* a Type-A midget submarine that was launched at 0333 and commanded by Ensign Sakamaki Kazuo with PO2C Inagaki Kiyoshi. *I-24* was attacked, rammed and sunk off Shemya Island, Aleutians in heavy fog by subchaser PC-487 in June 1943.

I-26

I-26 was the Japanese fleet submarine that was sent to the West Coast and sank the freighter *Cynthia Olson* 300 nautical miles off the coast of California at 0800 on December 7 (Hawaiian time) or 0900 in the time zone of the sinking. This was the first American ship to be sunk by a Japanese submarine in the war. *I-26* was sunk in the aftermath of the Battle of Samar off Leyte in October 1944. It was sunk by either USS *Coolbaugh* (DE-217) or USS *Richard M. Powell* (DE-403).

Imperial Japanese Navy (IJN)

The Imperial Japanese Navy, the *Nippon Kaigun* ("Navy of the Greater Japanese Empire"), was the third largest navy in the world at the beginning of the war (behind the British Royal Navy and the U.S. Navy).

"Infamy Speech"

The "Infamy Speech" was one of the most famous political speeches in American history. It was a 7-minute speech delivered by President Franklin D. Roosevelt to a Joint Session of Congress on December 8, 1941describing the Japanese attack on U.S. forces at Pearl Harbor, Hawaii. The speech was broadcast live by radio and attracted the largest audience in U.S. radio history, having been heard in more than 81% of American households.

Isokaze

The *Isokaze* ("Wind on the Beach"), was a *Kagerō*-class Japanese destroyer commissioned in November 1940 and part of the 17th Destroyer Division. It was attacked in April 1945 by aircraft of Task Force 58 about 150 miles southwest of Nagasaki, abandoned by the crew, and scuttled by gunfire from the *Yukikaze.*

Itaya, Shigeru (d. 1944)

Lieutenant Commander Shigeru Itaya was the first pilot airborne for the attack having launched from *Akagi.* He was killed in the Kuriles in July 1944.

President Roosevelt delivers his "Day of Infamy" speech to Congress on December 8, 1941. Behind him are Vice President Henry Wallace (left) and Speaker of the House Sam Rayburn. To the right, in uniform in front of Rayburn, is Roosevelt's son James, who escorted his father to the Capitol.

(National Archives)

* * *

USS *Jarvis* (DD-393)

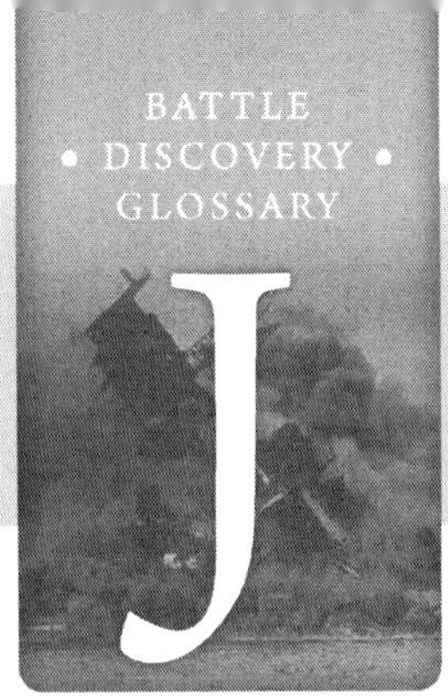

JN-19 code

The JN-19 code was the diplomatic consular-level code used by the Japanese and by which espionage activities in Hawaii were reported to Tokyo. It was read by the Americans and British but the keys were changed daily. It was not as complex as the diplomatic code Purple that was intercepted and readable by the decipher machine known as MAGIC. Nor was it as sophisticated as the Japanese naval code JN-25 in which operational messages were transmitted.

Japanese losses

The Japanese losses in the attack were relatively low. They lost a total of 29 aircraft missing in action or confirmed as crashed during the attack on Pearl Harbor—9 Mitsubishi Type Zero carrier-based fighters (*Reisen* or "Zero"), 15 Aichi Type 99 carrier-based bombers ("*KanBaku,*" later code-named "Val"), and 5 Nakajima Type 97 carrier-based attack bombers ("*KanKo,*" later code-named "Kate"). 5 Type A *Ko-hyoteki* Japanese midget submarines (Numbers *16,18, 19, 20, 22*)

Jarvis (DD-393)

The *Bagley*-class destroyer USS *Jarvis* was commissioned in 1937 and moored port side to *Mugford* at berth B-6 Navy Yard Pearl Harbor, during a restricted availability period; undamaged. *Jarvis* used anti-aircraft fire against attacking planes, made preparations to get underway, and sortied later in the morning on patrol. *Jarvis* was sunk by Japanese aircraft off Guadalcanal in August 1942.

Japanese losses were relatively few. A crashed Japanese "Zero" at Ft. Kamehameha

(U.S. Navy Photo #80-G-13040)

* * *

A Nakajima B5N1 "Kate" torpedo bomber on launch from the flight deck of a Japanese carrier ischeered on by crewmen as it heads for Pearl Harbor. The carrier is either the *Shōkaku* or *Zuikkaku.*

(National Archives photo)

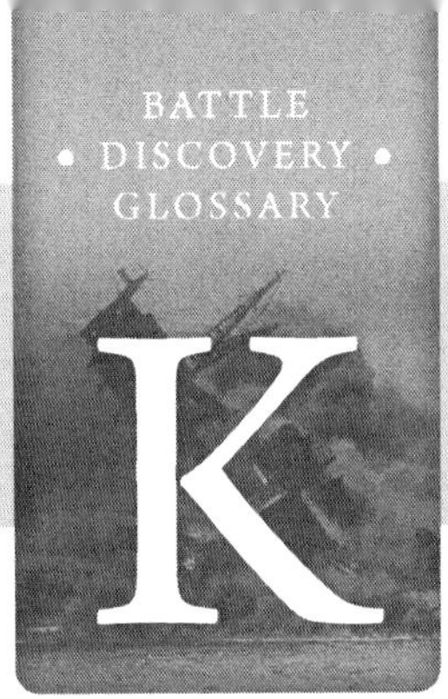

Kaaawa radar site

The Kaaawa radar site was 1 of the 5 (Fort Shafter, Kaawai, Kawailoa, Koko Head, Opana) air warning system radar sites used by the U.S. Army Signal Corps.

Kaigun

Kaigun is translated as "navy" and often refers to *Nihon Teikoku Kaigun,* "Japanese Imperial Navy."

Kaga

The Imperial Japanese Navy aircraft carrier *Kaga* ("Increased Joy") was launched in November 1921 and commissioned in 1929 but originally laid down as a battleship and restructured after the Washington Naval Conference. It was 1 of 6 Japanese carriers that participated in the attack (*Akagi, Kaga, Hiryū, Shōkaku, Sōryū, Zuikaku*). In the first wave, *Kaga* launched 9 Zero, 14 "Kates," and 12 "Kate" torpedo bombers and in the second wave, 9 "Zeroes" and 26 "Vals." During the 5 June 1942 Battle of Midway, *Kaga* was attacked and sunk by SBD2 "Dauntless" dive-bombers from the USS *Enterprise* and USS *Yorktown.*

Kagerō

The Japanese destroyer *Kagerō* ("Sun Haze") served as an escort vessel supporting the 6 IJN aircraft carriers. It was the first in its class of 19 destroyers that were fast warships with significant offensive armament potential and was commissioned in 1939. *Kagerō* was sunk in May 1943 by a mine and aircraft in Blackett Strait in the Solomon Islands 5 miles southeast of Rendova.

Kaneohe Bay Naval Air Station

Known today as Kaneohe Marine Corps Air Station, Kaneohe Naval Air Station was located northeast of Honolulu in a sheltered cove on the east coastline of Oahu and served as base for Navy Patrol Wing 1 which consisted on 36 PBY5 "Catalinas" and 1 OSU2 "Kingfisher" aircraft (VP-11, VP-12, VP-14). It was a new site with facilities still under construction and was a major Navy patrol seaplane base. Because of its location it was one of the first targets attacked, bombed, and strafed (5 minutes before Pearl Harbor). All the aircraft were damaged except for 3 that were on submarine patrol.

Kasumi

The Japanese destroyer *Kasumi* ("Haze") was commissioned in June 1939. It sailed as escort to the Strike Force guarding the fleet tankers. *Kasumi* was attacked by aircraft from Task Force 58 and scuttled in April 1945, 150 miles southwest of Nagasaki.

"Kate"
See Nakajima B5N2.

Kawailoa radar site
The site was 1 of the 5 (Fort Shafter, Kaawai, Kawailoa, Koko Head, Opana) air warning system radar sites used by the U.S. Army Signal Corps. Kawailoa, Kaawi, and Opana all detected aircraft on their SCR-270B mobile radar equipment that was being field tested and reported contact to the Information Center at Fort Shafter but the information was not interpreted as unusual.

***Keosanqua* (AT-38)**
The USS *Keosanqua* was an *Allegheny* class fleet tug commissioned in December 1920 that was operating at the harbor entrance with *Antares*. *Keosanqua* was undamaged in the attack.

Kenyo Maru
The *Kenyo Maru* was a converted Japanese merchant transport registered as a naval auxiliary vessel and oiler in September 1941. It was part of Supply Group One, sunk by USS *Whale* (SS-239) on 23 March 1943 about 120 miles northwest of Saipan.

KGMB
KGMB was one of 2 radio stations (KGU) on Oahu at the time of the attack. The station did not normally broadcast late at night but when aircraft were expected from the mainland, the Army Air Corps paid the station to remain on the air so

that incoming pilots had a radio beacon to assist in navigation. Approaching Japanese aircraft were also able to hear the station and were reassured at hearing music rather than alerts that the attack was still a surprise. At 0804 music was interrupted by a message recalling all military personnel to duty. At 1145 the station was ordered off the air by Army intelligence.

Kidō Butai

Kidō Butai ("Mobile Unit/Force" or "Strike Force") was not a formal name but, the convenient term and tactical designation for the Imperial Japanese Navy's 6-carrier battle group that attacked Pearl Harbor. It was also known as Carrier Striking Task Force.

Kimmel, Husband E. (1882–1958)

Admiral Husband E. Kimmel was commander of the Pacific Fleet homeported at Pearl Harbor. As Commander-in-Chief, Pacific, he favored an offensive role for the U.S. Navy against Japan and did not focus on defense at Pearl Harbor, viewing it as primarily an Army issue and under the purview of Lieutenant-General Walter C. Short. On November 27, Chief of Naval Operations Harold R. Stark cabled Kimmel with a war warning and ordering him to increase defensive preparations. Kimmel did so in part by sending *Lexington* and *Enterprise* to sea with aircraft to reinforce Midway Island and Wake Island respectively and he also conferred with Short. He was relieved of command on December 16, 1941 and a subsequent enquiry held him responsible for poor judgment. He was demoted to rear admiral and allowed to retire.

Kirishima

The Japanese battleship *Kirishima* was named for Mount Kirishima and commissioned in April 1915. It was 1 of 2 Japanese battleships (*Kirishima* and *Hiei*) that served as escorts for the 6-carrier strike force against Pearl Harbor. During the Second Battle of Guadalcanal in November 1942, *Kirishima* was disabled by gunfire from USS *Washington* (BB-56) and scuttled.

Koko Head radar site

The radar site was 1 of the 5 (Fort Shafter, Kaawai, Kawailoa, Koko Head, Opana) air warning system radar sites used by the U.S. Army Signal Corps.

Kokuyo Maru

Kokuyo Maru was a Japanese auxiliary oiler lanched in 1938 that served as part of Supply Group One. It was sunk by USS *Bonefish* (SS-223) on 30 July 1944.

Kukui (WAGL-225)

The *Kukui* was a U.S. Coast Guard *Manzanita*-class buoy tender constructed for the Lighthouse Service commissioned in August 1908 and moored at Pier 4 in Honolulu with *Reliance*. After the attack, *Kukui* transported a U.S. Army detachment to the island of Niihau after reports were received that a Japanese pilot (Shigenori Nishikaichi) had crash-landed on and taken control of the island. However, by the time *Kukui* arrived on 14 December local citizens had overpowered and killed the pilot. *Kukui* was decommissioned in February 1946.

Kuroshima, Kameto (1893–1965)
Captain Kameto Kuroshima was a senior staff officer to Admiral Yamamoto, who oversaw the planning of the Operation Hawaii attack (attack planner).

Kurusu, Saburo (1886–1954)
Saburo Kurusu was a Japanese career diplomat. Beginning November 15, 1941, he served as special envoy to the United States alongside Ambassador Kichisaburo Nomura, because Minister of Foreign Affairs Shigenori Togo did not have full trust in Ambassador Nomura. On the afternoon of December 7, 1941, Kurusu and Nomura delivered Japan's declaration of war against the United States after the Pearl Harbor attack had already occurred. He was interned at Hot Springs, Virginia, United States between December 1941 and June 1942 until an exchange of diplomatic personnel and civilians could be negotiated, at which time Kurusu was transported to Mozambique aboard passenger liner MS *Gripsholm* and then on to Japan.

Kusaka, Ryunosuke (1893–1971)
Ryunosuke Kusaka, was an Imperial Japanese Navy Rear Admiral at the time of the attack, Kusaka was then Chief of Staff of the First Air Fleet under Vice Admiral Chuichi Nagumo. He was part of the cadre of attack planners.

Kyokuto Maru

The *Kyokuto Maru* was a Japanese tanker and flagship of one of the 2 supply units for the First Air Fleet. It was sunk by USS *Bonefish* (SS-223) on July 30, 1944.

* * *

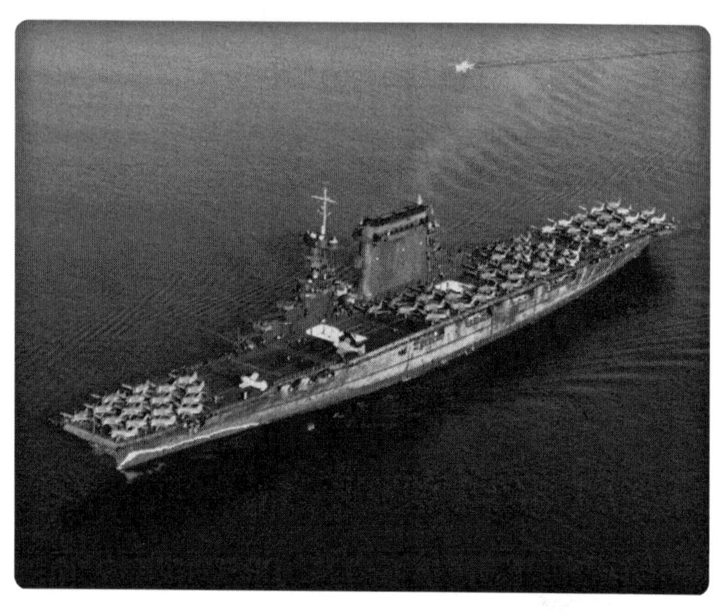

The USS *Lexington* (CV-2) leaving San Diego, California), on 14 October 1941. *Lexington* was at sea at the time of the attack.

(Official U.S. Navy photo 80-G-416362)

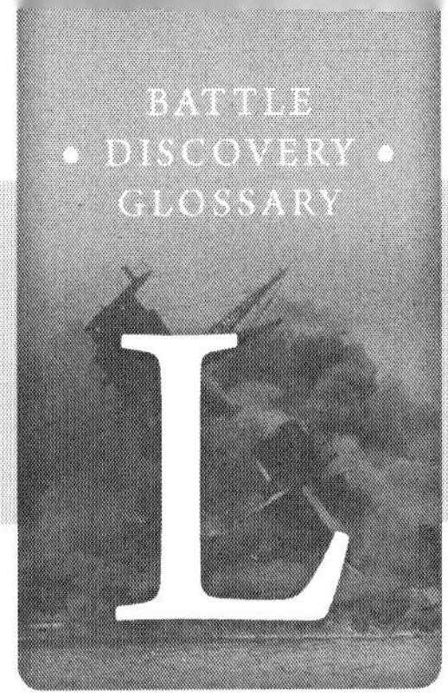

Lamberton (DMS-2)

The USS *Lamberton* was originally a *Wickes*-class destroyer (DD-119) commissioned in August 1918. On December 7, 1941, she was escorting USS *Minneapolis* to Oahu when the Japanese attacked Pearl Harbor.

Lamson (DD-367)

The USS *Lamson* was a *Mahan*-class destroyer commissioned in October 1936. Homeported at Pearl Harbor, *Lamson* was patrolling at sea when the attack occurred. *Lamson* served throughout the Pacific during the war and was subsequently sunk at Bikini Atoll in 1946 during the Operation Crossroads atomic weapons tests.

Lexington (CV-2)

The aircraft carrier USS *Lexington* was the lead ship in its class and commissioned in December 1922. *Lexington* was originally designed as a battlecruiser but changed to an aircraft carrier to meet requirements of the Washington Naval Treaty of 1922. *Lexington* was at sea ferrying aircraft to Midway Island at the time of the attack and a disappointment to Japanese planners and attackers who had hoped to find it at Pearl Harbor along with *Saratoga* (then en route to California) and *Enterprise* (returning from Wake Island). *Lexington* was sunk on May 8, 1942 during the Battle of the Coral Sea.

Lockard, Joseph L. (1922–2012)

Army private Joseph L. Lockard was 1 of 2 radar operators on duty at the Opana Mobile Radar Site. At 0702, he and Pvt. George Elliott saw a large radar echo blip on the screen and concluded that many aircraft were approaching Oahu from the north and were 132 miles out. They reported the contact to the temporary radar information center at Fort Shafter but it was mistakenly deemed to be a flight of 12 B-17s due to arrive from California rather than the first wave of Japanese aircraft.

Long (DD-209)

The USS *Long* was a *Clemson*-class destroyer commissioned in October 1919. On December 5, 1941, she departed Pearl Harbor as screen and escort for USS *Indianapolis* but returned on December 9th to commence antisubmarine patrols. *Long* was sunk by a kamikaze attack on 6 January 6, 1945 in Lingayen Gulf.

Two of the three "missing" carriers from Pearl Harbor that the Japanese hoped were in port. USS *Saratoga* (foreground) and USS *Lexington* (background) off Honolulu, Oahu, U.S. Territory of Hawaii, with Diamond Head in the background. Photo taken in February 1933.

(United States Navy Naval History and Heritage Command, Public Domain)

* * *

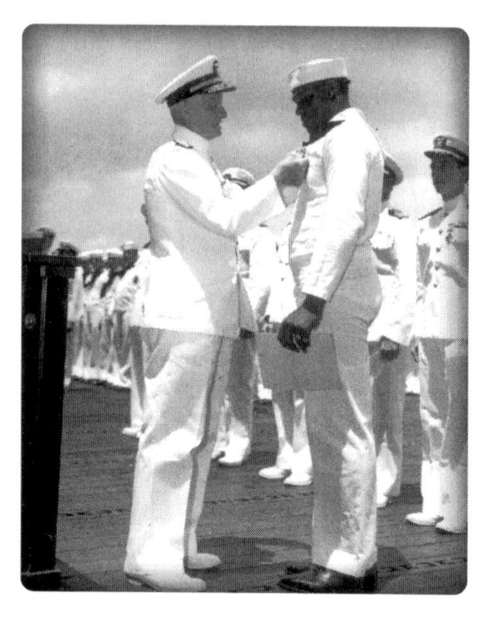

Admiral Chester W. Nimitz pins the Navy Cross on Doris Miller at a ceremony in Pearl Harbor, May 27, 1942.

(208-NP-8PP-2)

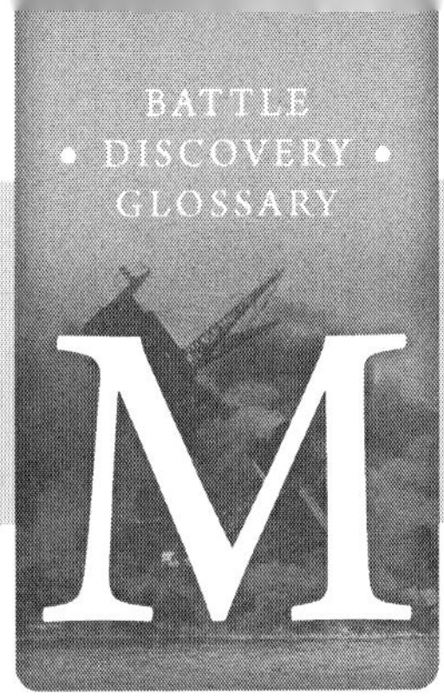

McDonald, Joseph P. (1919–1994)

Army private Joseph P. McDonald was the individual on duty at Fort Shafter who received the phone call from the Opana mobile radar site informing the Information Center: "There are a large number of planes coming in from the north 3 points east" as well as a subsequent one. McDonald passed the information to the temporary duty officer, Army Lieutenant Kemit Tyler, who believed the aircraft to be a formation of B-17s arriving from the West Coast. McDonald continued to serve throughout the Pacific during the war.

Macdonough (DD-351)

The USS *Macdonough* was a *Farragut*-class destroyer commissioned in March that 1935. *Macdonough* was at berth X-2, nested with *Dobbins*, *Hull*, *Dewey*, *Worden* and *Phelps*. Undamaged in the attack, the ship served throughout the Pacific during the war.

Mahan (DD-364)

The USS *Mahan* was the lead ship in its class and commissioned in September 1936. *Mahan* was at sea with Task Force 12 at the time of the attack. Three years to the day of the attack, on December 7, 1944, *Mahan* was patrolling the channel between Leyte and Ponyon Island and was struck by a kamikaze attack severely crippling the ship. Orders were issued to abandon ship and *Mahan* subsequently was sunk by torpedoes and gunfire from a U.S. Navy destroyer due to being unsalvageable.

Marine Air Group 21

Marine Air Group 21 at Ewa Field consisted of 11 Grumman F4F "Wildcat" fighters (the newest of USMC fighter planes at the time), 32 Scout dive-bombers and 6 utility planes. It was located 7 miles west of Pearl Harbor. On the day of the attack it was the first installation hit by the Japanese and all aircraft based there were destroyed. There were 17 casualties at the facility.

Marine Corps

See U.S. Marine Corps.

Marine railway dock

The marine railway dock located in Southeast Loch was built from 1918–1920 and had a capacity of 2,500 gross tons. It had a 332-ft wooden cradle for small ships and ways (rails) that ran 738 ft. It was used for handling destroyers, submarines, and smaller craft. At the time of the attack, minesweeper *Swan* was resting on the cradle.

Maryland (BB-46)

The USS *Maryland* was a *Colorado*-class battleship commissioned in July 1921 that was moored inboard of *Oklahoma* at berth F-5, forward of *Tennessee. Maryland* was damaged by two armor-piercing bomb hits that caused severe flooding. However, *Maryland* was the least damaged of the major ships. The Japanese erroneously reported that it had been sunk but it was repaired by February 1942 and returned to service in the Pacific and subsequently decommissioned in April 1947.

Matsuzaki, Mitsuo

Lieutenant Mitsuo Matsuzaki piloted the Nakajima B5N2 "Kate" of the 1st Attack Unit of the First Attack Wave in which the commander of the attack wave, Commander Mitsuo Fuchida, flew as attack leader and observer.

Medal of Honor

There were 15 recipients of the Congressional Medal of Honor award of which only 5 survived* the attack and 1 died in combat 11 months later: Mervyn S. Bennion, John W. Finn*, Edwin J. Hill, Francis C. Flaherty, Samuel G. Fuqua*, Herbert C. Jones, Isaac C. Kidd, Jackson C. Pharris*, Thomas J. Reeves, Donald K. Ross, Robert R. Scott, Peter Tomich, Franklin Van Valkenburgh, James R. Ward, Cassin Young (killed in action in Guadalcanal, November 1942)

Medusa (AR-1)

The USS *Medusa* was the first purpose-built repair ship for the U.S. Navy and was commissioned in 1924. During the attack it was moored Middle Loch south of Pearl City at berth X-23 near *Curtiss. Medussa* was undamaged and fired on midget submarine *No. 22* that subsequently was sunk by *Monaghan. Medusa* served throughout the war and was decommissioned in November 1946.

Merry Point Landing

Merry Point Landing is a small headland at the southeastern extremity of South East Loch. Personnel at the Fleet Landing at Merry Point (also, Merry's Point) were strafed by attacking Japanese aircraft.

Middle Loch

See Pearl Harbor.

Midget submarines

Midget submarines were used by the Japanese in the attack. Several hours prior to the attack 5 Type A *Ko-hyoteki* Japanese midget submarines (Numbers *16,18, 19, 20, 22*) were launched against Pearl Harbor. They had hull numbers but no names and are most often referred to by the hull number of the submarine that carried and launched them (though in some circumstances, they are known by their own hull number as in the case of *No. 19* (also known as *Ha-19*) launched by *1-24*. Thus the midget submarine from *I-16* was known as

I-16 tou ("*tou*" meaning "boat"). The submarines had a crew of two men, a junior officer who conned the boat and a petty officer who controlled ballast, trim, and diving. Submarines were 78.5 feet long with a displacement of 46 tons. For the attack they carried 2 Type 97 specially modified torpedoes. Of the 5 boats *No. 19* was grounded and captured on the east side of Oahu along with one of the crewmembers, Kazo Sakamaki (1918–1999), who became the first Japanese prisoner of war. Boat *No. 18* was sunk by a depth charge near the harbor entrance. Boat *No. 20* was attacked and sunk by the USS *Ward* (DD-139) at 0637 several miles from the entrance. Boat *No. 22* entered the harbor and fired torpedoes at USS *Curtiss* (AV-4) and USS *Monaghan* (DD-354) but missed both and probably hit a dock at Pearl City and Ford Island. *Monaghan* sank *No. 22* at 0843. The final sub, *No. 16,* has yet to be found. It is believed that *No. 16* successfully entered Pearl Harbor and fired torpedoes at Battleship Row perhaps hitting the USS *Oklahoma.* There is photographic evidence supporting this theory wherein water spray in the shape of a "rooster tail" is seen in the photograph, suggesting a midget submarine rocking up and down due to the launching of a torpedo in the shallow water.

Mikawa, Gunichi (1888–1981)

Vice Admiral Mikawa Gunichi commanded Battleship Division 3 and led the first section consisting of battleships *Hiei* and *Kirishima* as support and escort during the attack.

Minneapolis (CA-36)

The USS *Minneapolis* was a *New Orleans*-class cruiser commissioned in May 1934. *Minneapolis* was at sea at the time of the attack and immediately took up patrol and served with distinction throughout the war. The ship was decommissioned in 1947.

Miller, Doris (1919–1943)

U.S. Navy Mess Attendant Third Class Doris "Dorie" Miller was serving aboard *West Virginia* at the time of the attack. He was the first African American to receive the Navy Cross for bravery in assisting and evacuating the wounded and dead, including the ship's captain, and for manning an anti-aircraft gun. He was considered one the heroes of the attack. He was killed aboard the *Liscome Bay* after it was torpedoed during the Battle of Makin Island on November 24, 1943.

Mitsubishi A6M2

The Mitsubishi A6M2 "Zeke" or "Zero," was a carrier-borne fighter with a single pilot that carried 1 60-kg (132-lb) bomb under each wing and had a speed of 340 mph (544 kph) and range of 1,160 miles (1867 km). Nine were lost during the attack, 3 during the first wave and 6 during the second wave out of 43 and 35 respectively.

Monaghan (DD-353)

The last of the *Farragut*-class destroyers, the USS *Monahan* was commissioned in April 1935. She was a ready-duty destroyer and minutes before the attack was ordered to sea in response to *Ward*'s sighting of a submarine. Before getting underway, the attack began. *Monaghan* sank midget submarine *No. 22* at 0843 after ramming it and dropping 2 depth charges. This came after after *No. 22* had fired torpedoes at *Monaghan*. The ship served in the Pacific until foundering in Typhoon Cobra on 18 December 1944.

Montgomery (DM-17)

The USS *Montgomery* was a high-speed minelayer (converted destroyer), moored in berth D-3, Middle Loch, in nest with division, order of ships from starboard *Ramsay*, *Breese*, *Montgomery*, and *Gamble*. *Montgomery* was undamaged in the attack. *Montgomery* was originally commissioned in 1921 as a *Wickes*-class destroyer. After serving in the Pacific throughout the war, the ship was decommissioned in April 1945.

Morimasu, Tadashi

See Takeo Yoshikawa.

Mugford (DD-389)

The *Bagley*-class destroyer USS *Mugford* was commissioned in August 1937 and moored port side to the *Sacramento*, in berth B-6, at the Navy Yard. *Mugford* was undamaged in the attack. The ship continued to serve throughout the war and was decommissioned in August 1946.

Murata, Shigigeharu
Lieutentant Commander Shigigeharu Murata was the leader of the "Kate" torpedo bombers of the first wave from the *Akagi*.

USS *Maryland* and capsized USS *Oklahoma*

(U.S. Navy Photo #80-G-19949 National Archives)

* * *

USS *Nevada* (BB-36) beached and burning at 0925 hours after her attempt to exit the harbor. Hit by Japanese bombs and torpedoes, she was beached at Hospital Point to prevent her sinking and blocking the channel. The harbor tugboat *Hoga* (YT-146) is alongside *Nevada*'s port bow, helping to fight fires.

(National Archives photo)

Nagano, Osami (1880–1947)
Admiral and Chief of the Japanese Naval General Staff Osami Nagano was the senior naval officer during most of the war. He was opposed to Admiral Yamamoto's plans to attack Pearl Harbor but gave his approval after Yamamoto threatened to resign as Combined Fleet commander. Nagano was tried for war crimes after the war and died of a heart attack before the conclusion of his trial.

Nagumo, Chuichi (1887–1944)
Vice Admiral Nagumo was commander of the First Air Fleet despite a lack of experience with and knowledge of airpower. During the attack he commanded from his flagship *Akagi* with Commander Minoru Genda serving as his air adviser and was later criticized for not launching an unplanned third attack wave. He was later in command of the Japanese air fleet during the Battle of Midway and on July 6, 1944, during the final phase of the Battle of Saipan, Nagumo committed suicide as a result of his failure to hold Saipan as its military commander.

Nakajima B5N2

Known as the "Kate," the Nakajima B5N2 was a carrier-borne (primarily) single-engine torpedo bomber, 1 18- inch (28 cm) torpedo or 1 500-kg (1100-lb) bomb, maximum speed of 235 mphm(378 kph), range of 1237 miles (1992 km), crew of two or three, service ceiling 27,100 ft (8,260 m) (1 pilot, 1 commander, 1 back gunner/radio operator). The B5N2 carried Commander Mitsuo Fuchida, the commander of the attack on Pearl Harbor. A "Kate" from the carrier *Hiryū* was credited with sinking the battleship *Arizona.* There were 79 "Kates" in the First Wave of the attack with 5 losses and 54 in the Second Wave.

Nakajima E8N

Codenamed by Allied intelligence as "Dave," the Nakajima E8N was a catapult-launched biplane and floatplane used for reconnaissance. They were launched from *Chikuma* and *Tone* during the attack.

Narwhal (SS-167)

The USS *Narwhal* was a submarine commissioned in 1927 and the lead of its class. It was moored at berth S-9 next to *Gudgeon* at the Submarine Base and was undamaged in the attack. *Narwhal*'s gunners assisted in the downing of 2 aircraft. *Narwhal* served in the Pacific throughout the war and was decommissioned in April 1945.

Neosho (AO-23)

The *Cimarron*-class fleet oiler USS *Neosho* was commissioned in August 1939 and moored forward of *Maryland* and *Oklahoma* and aft of *California. Neosho* was undamaged in the attack and moved to berth M-3 Merry Point at 0930. *Neosho* was sunk during the Battle of the Coral Sea on May 11, 1942 after an initial attack on it several days earlier.

Nevada (BB-36)

The USS *Nevada* was the lead battleship in a class of 2 along with *Oklahoma.* Commissioned in March 1916, *Nevada* was moored aft of *Arizona* at mooring quay F-8 in Battleship Row but not alongside others ships and was thus able to maneuver and got underway through the leadership and efforts of Lieutenant Commander Francis J. Thomas, who was senior officer and Ensign Joseph K. Taussig, Jr., because the captain, F. W. Scanland, was ashore. Seriously damaged in the attack during both waves, *Nevada* got underway but beached at Hospital Point. *Nevada* suffered a total of 60 killed and 109 wounded. The ship was refloated and repaired and subsequently completed major overhaul after which *Nevada* served on convoy duty in the Atlantic Ocean. She participated in the D-Day Normandy landings on June 6, 1944. She was subsequently damaged in a kamikaze attack at Okinawa in late March 1945 and decommissioned in August 1946.

New Orleans (CA-32)

The heavy cruiser USS *New Orleans* was commissioned in February 1934 and the lead in its class. She was moored at berth B-16 at Navy Yard Pearl Harbor undergoing engineering repairs and received minor damage. The crew returned anti-aircraft fire and ammunition was passed manually because there was no electrical power for the ammunition hoists. Observing this was ship's chaplain Lieutenant Howell M. Forgy, who encouraged them with the words "praise the Lord and pass the ammunition." The ship served throughout the Pacific Ocean during the remainder of the war and was decommissioned in February 1947.

Niihau Incident

This unusual event occurred on December 7, 1941 after Airman 1st Class Shigenori Nishikaichi flying in second wave of attack in his "Zero" fighter was attacked by P-36As and had a fuel tank punctured by a bullet. Badly leaking fuel, he made an emergency landing on the sparsely-populated island of Niihau, the western most of the Hawaiian Islands, with the intent of waiting for an IJN submarine to rescue him in accordance with emergency plans. Unaware of the attack, Howard Kaleohano, a local resident rushed to help. He took the pilot's papers and pistol and hefted him away from the wreck and called on others to help communicate with the pilot. The first to do so, though unwillingly, was Ishimatsu Shintani, who spoke briefly to the pilot and left. Yoshio Harada, a second generation Japanese American and his wife, Irene, spoke to the pilot and were informed by him of the attack but they did not tell others. By evening, radio reports were received and islanders took Nishikaichi into custody and awaited arrival of authorities. On December 12th at 4 o'clock Shintani spoke to Kaleohano and tried to buy the pilot's papers and for $200.00 but the offer was refused. With maritime traffic curtailed the authorities did not arrive immediately and during the interim Nishikaichi convinced Harada to help him escape. Not waiting for Shintani's return, Harada and Nishikaichi overpowered one guard and put him in a warehouse (the other guards were absent)." They then took the pilot's pistol and a shotgun which were in the warehouse and went to Kaleohano's house but he hid, fled, warned others, and paddled with 5 others in a lifeboat for 10 hours to Kaua'i for help. During this time Harada and Nishikaichi captured a small group of residents, among them Kaahakila Kalimahuluhulu, known as Kalima, and Benenhakaka "Ben" Kanahele and his wife "Ella." Sensing fatigue in the captor's, Ben and Ella attacked them and during the struggle Ben was shot 3 times by Nishikaichi but Ben and Ella killed him whereupon Harada turned the shotgun on himself and committed suicide. Kanahele later received a Purple Heart and Medal for Merit (though Ella received nothing). Shintani was sent to an internment camp and Irene Harada was held in custody for 31 months but never charged. During this time Nishikaichi was allowed to stay with the Haradas although four guards also were placed at the house. The incident showed the potential for ethnic and racial allegiance to be a factor in the war and may have been a factor in the decision to inter over 120,000 Japanese Americans during the war through the presidential executive order 9066, signed by President Roosevelt.

Nippon Maru

The *Nippon Maru* (or *Nihon Maru*) was a fleet oil tanker and part of Supply Group 2. It was later sunk by USS *Scamp* (SS-277) on January 14, 1944.

Nishikaichi, Shigenori (1919–1922)

Airman First Class Nishikaichi flew an A6M2 "Zero" that made an emergency landing on Niihau and was the center of what is known as the Niihau Incident. He was killed on December 12th in a struggle with other islanders.

Nomura, Kichisaburō (1877–1964)

Kichisaburō Nomura was a retired Admiral (1937) in the Imperial Japanese Navy and the ambassador to the United States at the time of the attack. On the afternoon of December 7, 1941, Special Envoy Saburo Kurusu and Nomura delivered Japan's declaration of war against the United States after the Pearl Harbor attack had already occurred.

Northampton (CA-26)

The *Chester*-class heavy cruiser USS *Northampton* was commissioned in May 1930 and at sea with *Enterprise* at the time of the attack. *Northampton* was strafed by a Japanese "Zero" near Kauai. *Northampton* was sunk at the night Battle of Tassafaronga on November 30, 1942 during the Guadalcanal Campaign.

Shigenori Nishikaichi, the pilot who became the center of the Niihau Incident

(Unknown source)

* * *

Battleship Row seen from the capsized USS *Oglala*.

(U.S. Navy History and Heritage Command photo)

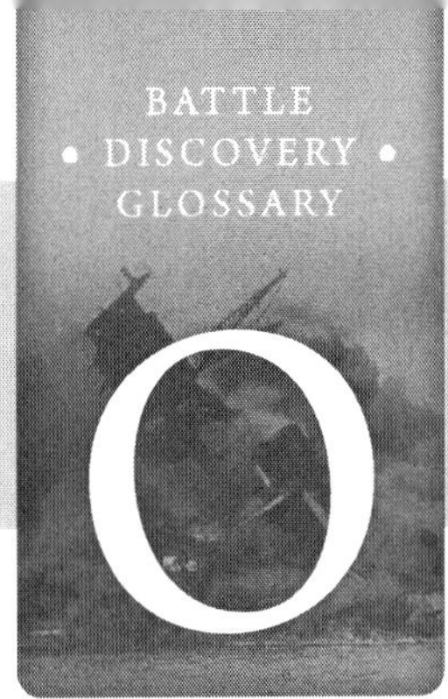

Oahu

Oahu is the third largest of the islands of Hawaii and was the site attacks on December 7,1941 of military installations throughout the island. The primary attack was on U.S. Navy ships and facilities at Pearl Harbor, a lagoon harbor with a southward-facing entrance that also encompasses Ford Island, an islet at the center of Pearl Harbor. According to the 1940 census, a year before the attack, the population of Oahu was 257,000 excluding military personnel. Two volcanic ranges (Waianae and Koolau) run north and south through the island and this geography and topography created paths for the air strikes that ran down the center of the island and along the east and west coasts.

Oglala (CM-4)

The USS *Oglala* was a cruiser-minelayer originally built as a commercial vessel and subsequently purchased and commissioned by the Navy in 1917. *Oglala* was moored alongside *Helena* at berth B-2; Damaged by torpedo hit on *Helena*, capsized and sunk but salvaged and recommissioned as engine-repair ship and returned to service in February 1944, serving in the South Pacific until being decommissioned in July 1946.

Oil embargo

An oil embargo of shipments to Japan by the United States became part of the impetus for Japan going to war with the U.S. The economic event occurred on July 26, 1941 when President Franklin Roosevelt froze all Japanese assets in the United States in retaliation for the Japanese occupation of French Indo-China and on August 1 established an embargo on oil and gasoline exports to Japan. Britain and the Dutch East Indies followed soon after with the result of Japan losing 88% of its imported oil (80% coming from the U.S.) and much of its overseas trade. Japan's oil reserves were only sufficient to last three years and much less if it went to war. Japan's immediate response was to occupy Saigon (with Vichy France's acquiescence) and attempt control of Southeast Asia, including Malaya (after the Pearl Harbor attack). This would mean control of the region's rubber and tin production, much of which was imported by the West. These actions and others were part of the Japanese economic calculations of whether or not to go to war. At the same time, diplomatic negotiations were being carried out between Japan and the United States but these came to a stalemate in November 1941.

Oklahoma (BB-37)

The USS *Oklahoma* was a *Nevada*-class battleship commissioned in May 1917. She was moored in Battleship Row, outboard of *Maryland* at mooring quay F-5, forward of *West Virginia*. *Oklahoma* was hit early and hard in the attack, ultimately by 9 torpedoes. Within minutes she began to list heavily and capsized with a loss of 415 sailors and 14 Marines. Many of the crewmembers were trapped inside the capsized ship and 32 were cut out and rescued although after 3 days no more sounds were heard from within. The ship was a total loss. Salvaging operations began in July 1942. In March 1943 the process of righting (parbuckling) the ship began and was completed by June 1943 and unrecovered remains were removed. By December 1943, *Oklahoma* was placed in dry dock and armaments, superstructure, and equipment were removed. The ship was decommissioned in September 1944 and sold to a salvage company for $46,000 but during transit to California, it sank in a storm while being towed by 2 tugs.

Omori, Sentaro (1892–1974)

Rear Admiral (later, Vice Admiral) Omori was the commander of Destroyer Division 1 at the time of the attack.

Onishi, Takijiro (1891–1945)
Rear Admiral Onishi was tasked by Admiral Yamamoto to conduct the feasibility study of an attack on Pearl Harbor. Commander Minoru Genda served under him and was the key staff officer creating the attack plan. Onishi committed suicide after the Japanese surrender in August 1945.

***Ontario* (AT-13)**
The ocean-going tug USS *Ontario* was commissioned in September 1912. *Ontario* was moored in berth B-18, Repair Basin, Pearl Harbor outboard of the *Sicard* and undergoing an overhaul. It was undamaged in the attack and returned fire against the Japanese aircraft. The tug served in the Pacific throughout the war and was decommissioned in June 1946.

Opana Mobile Radar Site
The Opana Mobile Radar site was 1 of 6 mobile radar sites that served as Signal Corps, U.S. Army air warning system for air defense of the Hawaiian Islands. The air warning system information center was at Fort Shafter, Oahu. Located several hundred feet above sea level, the Opana site consisted of several tents and 2 mobile trailers and was considered the best of the sites. The radars were model SCR-270B.

Opana Point
Opana Point is the northern tip of Oahu and site of radar equipment manned by Privates George Elliott and Joseph Lockhard. They received an echo contact on the screen at 0702

and reported it to the Information Center a few minutes later, but it was mistakenly thought to be the flight of 12 B-17s arriving from California rather than the first wave of attacking Japanese aircraft that consisted of more than 50 aircraft (a fact not passed on to the Information Center at Fort Shafter).

"Operation Hawaii"
This phrase was the Japanese Imperial General Headquarters code name for the attack on Hawaii (also called "Hawaii Operation" and "Operation AI"). During the planning stages it was known as "Operation Z."

"Operation Z"
See "Operation Hawaii" above.

* * *

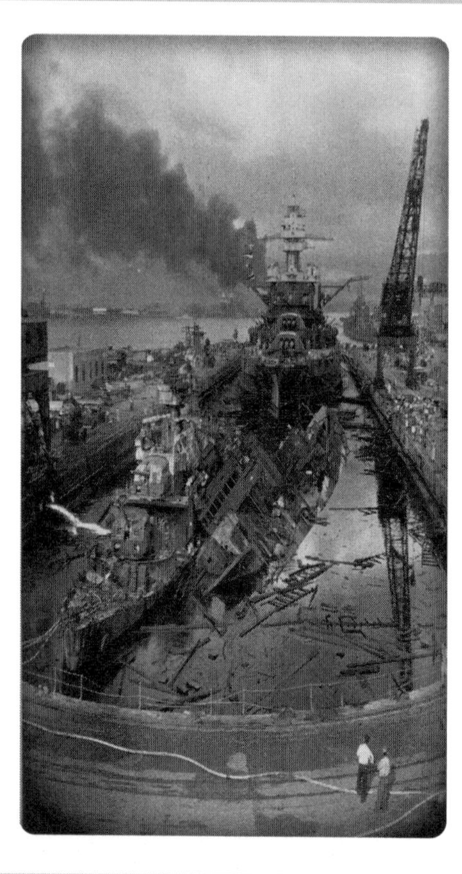

The wrecked destroyers *Downes* (DD-375) left, and *Cassin* (DD-372), right, in Drydock One at the Pearl Harbor Navy Yard, soon after the end of the Japanese air attack. *Cassin* has capsized against *Downes. Pennsylvania* (BB-38) is astern, occupying the rest of the drydock.

(Official U.S. Navy photo # 80-G-19943)

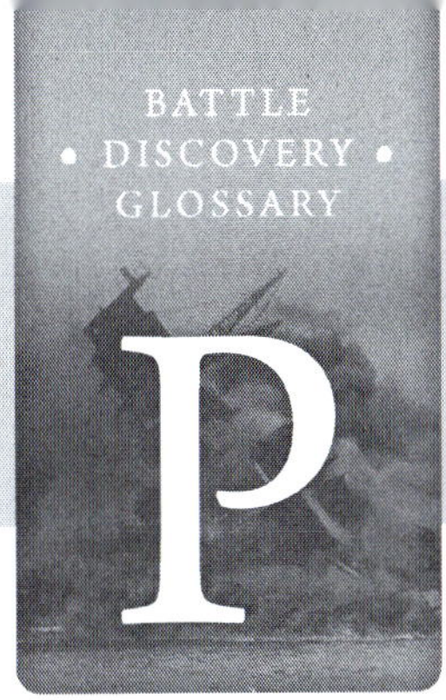

P-26 Peashooter
See Boeing P-26 "Peashooter."

P-36 Hawk
See Curtiss P-36 "Hawk."

P-40 Warhawk
See Curtiss P-40C "Warhawk."

Patrol Wing One
Patrol Wing One consisted of three squadrons (VP-11, 12, 16) with a total of 36 functional aircraft stationed at Kaneohe Naval Air Station on the east side of Oahu. Of these, 33 were present and all were damaged or destroyed. There were 17 members killed and 13 seriously wounded.

Patrol Wing Two
Patrol Wing Two consisted of 3 squadrons (VP-22, 23, 24) with a total of 38 planes stationed at the seaplane facilities at Ford Island Naval Air Station of which 33 were damaged or destroyed.

Patterson (DD-392)

The *Bagley*-class destroyer USS *Patterson* was commissioned in 1937 and moored at berth X-11 with *Henley* and *Ralph Talbot*. Undamaged in the attack, *Patterson* returned fire against Japanese aircraft. *Patterson* served throughout the Pacific during the war and was decommissioned in November 1945.

PBY

See Consolidated PBY-5A.

PBY 4

See Consolidated PBY-5A.

Pearl City

Pearl City is located on the north shore of Pearl Harbor.

Pearl Harbor

Pearl Harbor is a natural lagoon harbor on the south shore of Oahu with Ford Island setting in the center of it was the homeport of the U.S. Pacific Fleet in 1941. Pearl Harbor was originally an extensive shallow embayment known by the Hawaiians as *Wai Momi* ("Waters of Pearl") or *Pu'uloa* ("Long Hill"). In Hawaiian legends, *Pu'uloa* was the home of the shark goddess, Ka'ahupahau, and her brother (or son), Kahi'uka. According to legend, Keaunui, the head of the Ewa chiefs, cut is a navigable channel near the present Pu'uloa salt-works, making by the estuary, known as "Pearl River," accessible to navigation by widening and deepening it. Pearl Harbor is configured like a triangle with the apex pointing south and providing the entrance. In the middle of the harbor is Ford Island and to its north there is a peninsula on which Pearl City is built. The water to east of the peninsula is Middle Loch and to the east is East Loch with Aiea Bay situated to the far east. Southeast of Ford Island is Southeast Loch. Beyond Middle Loch is another peninsula, Waipio Peninsula and to the west of it is West Loch. Both East Loch and Middle Loch were filled with ships at anchorage.

Pelias (AS-14)

The *Griffin*-class submarine tender USS *Pelias* was commissioned in September 1941 and moored at the Submarine Base dock. *Pelias* was undamaged and served in the Pacific throughout the war from its homeport in Freemantle, Australia. *Pelias* was decommissioned in June 1970.

Pennsylvania (BB-38)

The USS *Pennsylvania* was the lead ship in its class of battleships and was commissioned in June 1916. At the time of the attack, *Pennsylvania*, serving at the Pacific Fleet flagship, was in Dry Dock No. 1, along with *Cassin* and *Downes* and was damaged by strafing and bombing, especially during the second wave. One of the first ships to return fire, there were 24 men killed (including the Executive Officer), 14 missing in action, and 38 wounded. *Pennsylvania*, underwent repairs until March 1942 and then served in the Pacific until the end of the war. *Pennsylvania* was used as a target ship during the atomic bomb testing at Bikini Atoll in July 1946 and was subsequently sunk in February 1948.

Perry (DMS-17)

The USS *Perry* was originally a *Clemson*-class destroyer (DD-340) commissioned in August 1922. *Perry* was redesignated a high-speed minelayer (DMS-17) effective November 1940. At the time of the attack, *Perry* was moored at buoy D-7, in the following order from north: *Trever*, *Wasmuth*, *Zane*, and *Perry*. *Perry* was undamaged in the attack and was credited with downing 1 aircraft before beginning minesweeping duties and patrol. *Perry* was sunk in enemy action on 13 September 1944 near Angaur (Palau).

Phelps (DD-360)

The *Porter*-class destroyer USS *Phelps* was commissioned in February 1946 and moored at berth X-2 undergoing tender overhaul, nested with *Hull*, *Dewey*, *Worden*, *Macdonough*, and *Dobbins*. Undamaged in the attack, *Phelps* was credited with shooting down one aircraft during the attack before getting underway and joining *Blue*, *Monaghan*, and *St. Louis* in creating an anti-submarine screen. *Phelps* served in the Pacific and Atlantic theaters and was decommissioned in November 1945.

Phoenix (CL-46)

The *Brooklyn*-class light cruiser USS *Phoenix* was commissioned in October 1938 and moored at berth C-6. *Phoenix* was undamaged in the attack and got underway quickly to join other ships in the unsuccessful search for the Japanese aircraft carriers. *Phoenix* served throughout the Pacific and was decommissioned in 1946. The ship was sold to Argentina in 1951 and became the *General Belgrano* and was sunk in battle by HMS *Conqueror* on May 2, 1982 during the Falklands War.

Porter (DD-356)

USS *Porter* was the lead ship in its class and commissioned in October 1936. On December 5th, Porter left Pearl Harbor with *Lexington*'s Task Force 12 to deliver Marines and aircraft to Midway Island and was at sea during the attack at Pearl Harbor. *Porter* was sunk following enemy action on October 26, 1942 but there is historical uncertainty as to whether it was from a torpedo fired by a Japanese submarine *I-21* or from an errant torpedo of a ditching U.S. TBF "Avenger."

Portland (CA-33)

USS *Portland* was the lead ship in its class of cruisers and was commissioned in February 1943. At the time of the attack, *Portland* was 2 days out of Pearl Harbor en route to Midway Island with *Lexington*. The ship served throughout the Pacific Theater and was decommissioned in July 1946.

"Praise the Lord and pass the ammunition."

As crewmembers of *New Orleans* fired 5-inch anti-aircraft shells at Japanese aircraft and struggled to manually pass ammunition and operate the gun, the ship's chaplain, Lieutentant Howell M. Forgy encouraged them with the words "praise the

Lord and pass the ammunition." Reports of this spread and the words were put to music with the same title by Frank Loesser. By December 1942, the song was in the number 2 popularity position, just behind Bing Crosby's "White Christmas."

Preble (DM-20)

USS *Preble* was originally a *Clemson*-class destroyer (DD-345) commissioned in March 1920 and subsequently designated a high-speed minelayer. *Preble* was moored in berth B-15, undergoing scheduled overhaul with no weapons onboard. Nested order of ships from the pier outboard was *Tracy*, *Preble*, and *Cummings*. Undamaged in the attack, *Preble* served throughout the Pacific and was decommissioned in December 1945.

Pruitt (DM-22)

USS *Pruitt* was a high-speed minelayer that was originally commissioned in June 1920 as a *Clemson*-class destroyer (DD-347). *Pruitt* was moored at berth B-18, Navy Yard, undergoing routine overhaul with *Sicard* and *Ontario* moored to port in that order. The ship was undamaged in the attack and continued to serve until being decommissioned in December 1945.

PT Boats

PT boats were present at the attack from Motor Torpedo Boat Squadron 1, which had 12 boats homeported at Pearl Harbor, all of which opened fire with .50-caliber machine guns on the attacking aircraft. PTs 20, 21, 22, 23, 24, and 25, were moored at the Pearl Harbor Submarine Base in three nests of two. Across

Southeast Loch from the Submarine Base, about halfway to Ford Island, the other 6 boats of the squadron (26, 27, 28, 29, 30, 42) were being loaded aboard the *Ramapo* for shipment to the Philippines. PTs 27, 29, 30, and 42 were in cradles resting on the *Ramapo*'s deck. PTs 26 and 28 were in cradles on the dock beneath, awaiting hoisting aboard the *Ramapo.*

Pyro (AE-1)

The USS *Pyro* was an ammunition ship originally commissioned in 1920. Decommissioned in 1924, the ship was commissioned a second time in July 1939. *Pyro* was moored starboard side to West Loch dock and sustained minor damage due to a near miss from a dive-bomber. The ship continued to serve in the Pacific throughout the war and was decommissioned in June 1946.

* * *

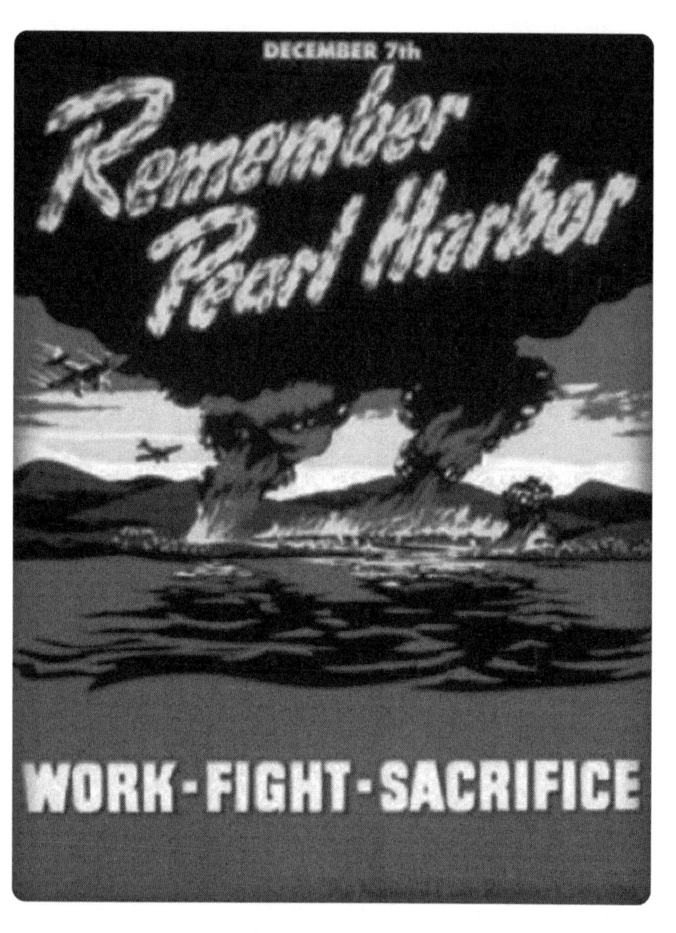

"Remember Pearl Harbor" slogan for wartime posters

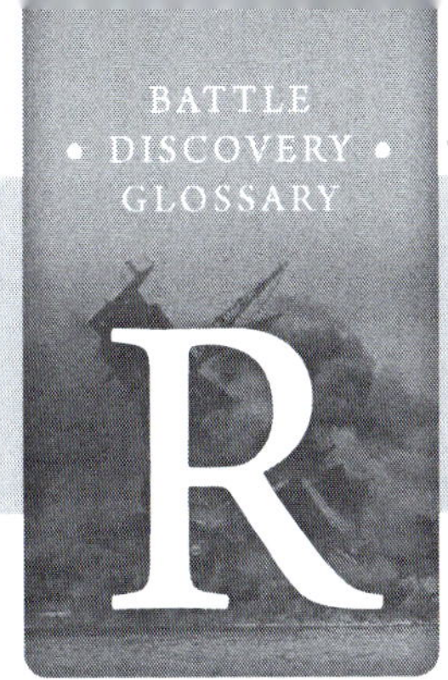

Rail (AM-26)

The USS *Rail* was a *Lapwing*-class minesweeper commissioned in June 1918 and moored in a nest at the Coal Dock with *Turkey*, *Bobolink*, and *Vireo.* Undamaged in the attack, *Rail* returned fire with its 50-calbre guns. The ship served throughout the Pacific and was decommissioned in February 1946.

Raliegh (CL-7)

The *Omaha*-class light cruiser USS *Raliegh* was commissioned in February 1924 and moored at berth F-12 forward of *Utah* and aft of *Detroit. Raliegh* was damaged by one torpedo in the first attack wave. *Raliegh* returned to service in February 1942. The ship served in the Pacific and extensively in the Aleutian Islands campaign and was decommissioned in November 1945.

Ralph Talbot (DD-390)

The USS *Ralph Talbot* was a *Bagley*-class destroyer commissioned in October 1937 and moored in East Loch bow to southward to buoy X-11 with the *Patterson* alongside to port and the *Henley* to starboard. The ship was undamaged and credited with downing one aircraft before getting underway at 0900 for anti-submarine patrol. Serving in the Pacific throughout the war, the ship was damaged in August 1942 in action off Savo Island and after the war was decommissioned in August 1946.

Ramapo **(AO-12)**

The USS *Ramapo* was a *Pakota*-class fleet oiler commissioned in November 1919 and moored in berth B-12, aft of *Rigel* and in the process of loading PT boats that were being sent to the Philippines. *Ramapo* was undamaged and continued service in the Pacific Theater and area of the Aleutian Islands until the war's end and decommissioning in January 1946.

Ramsay **(DM-16)**

The USS *Ramsay* was originally a *Wickes*-class destroyer (DD-124) that was first commissioned in February 1919 and subsequently converted to a high-speed minelayer and reclassified in June 1930. *Ramsay* was moored in berth D-3, Middle Loch, in nest with its division. The order of ships from starboard was: *Ramsay*, *Breese*, *Montgomery*, and *Gamble. Ramsay* was undamaged in the attack, served throughout the war, and was decommissioned in October 1945.

Ramsey, Logan C. (1898–1972)

Lieutenant Commander (later, Rear Admrial) Ramsey, Operations Officer of Patrol Wing Two, ordered at 0758 that a naval message be sent to "all ships present at Hawaiin [sic] area" after watching a low-flying Japanese plane drop a bomb on Ford Island. In his testimony before a Joint Committee of Congress investigating the attack he stated that after seeing a bomb detonate: "I dashed across the hall into the radio room, ordered a broadcast in plain English on all frequencies, 'Air Raid, Pearl Harbor. This is no drill.' The detonation of the bomb dropped by that first plane was my first positive knowledge of an enemy attack."

Reedbird (AMc-30)

The USS *Reedbird* was built in 1935 as a wooden purse-seiner and purchased by the Navy in 1940 for use as a coastal minesweeper. Undamaged in the attack, *Reedbird* operated in Hawaiian waters throughout the war before being deactivated in January 1946.

Reid (DD-369)

The USS *Reid* was a *Mahan*-class destroyer commissioned in November 1936 and nested with *Conyngham*, *Tucker*, *Case* and *Selfridge*, undergoing repairs alongside *Whitney* at berth X-8. *Reid* was undamaged in the attack and served in the Pacific Theater until being attacked, struck, and sunk by kamikaze aircraft on December 11, 1944.

Reliance (WSC-150)

The USCG *Reliance* was a U.S. Coast Guard *Active*-class patrol boat commissioned in August 1927 and moored at Pier 4 in Honolulu with *Kukui*. Undamaged in the attack, *Reliance* served throughout the war in anti-submarine patrol duties and was decommissioned in August 1947.

"Remember Pearl Harbor!"

"Remember Pearl Harbor!" became a popular slogan after the attack that was used for recruiting, propaganda, and support for the American war effort. Evoking memories of the earlier slogans "Remember the Alamo!" and "Remember the *Maine*!" the exhortation was also the title of one of the first movies to address the attack. It was filmed by Republic Pictures in 1942 and starred Don "Red" Barry (1912–1980).

Rigel (AR-11)

The USS *Rigel* was an *Altair*-class destroyer tender and repair ship, commissioned in February 1922 and moored in berth B-13 at the Navy Yard. *Rigel* was unarmed and undergoing major repairs and conversion, forward of *Ramapo*. The ship received minor damage from bomb near misses and her crew quickly assisted in rescue operations. The ship served in the South Pacific for the remainder of the war and was decommissioned in July 1946.

Roberts Commission

The Roberts Commission was a presidentially-appointed fact-finding commission created to investigate the attack on Pearl Harbor. Its named was derived from the head of the commission, U.S. Supreme Court Associate Justice Owen Josephus Roberts (1875–1955). Its investigation concluded that Admiral Husband E. Kimmel and Lieutenant General Walter C. Short were guilty of "dereliction of duty" with respect to their preparations for potential attack by the Japanese. There was a subsequent commission with the same name and head (though formally known as the American Commission for the Protection and Salvage of Artistic and Historic Monuments in War Areas) from 1943–46 that was created to help the U.S. Army protect cultural works in Allied-occupied areas of Europe

Roosevelt, Franklin D. (1882–1945)
President Roosevelt was president when the attack occurred and had been so for 9 years. On the day of the attack President Roosevelt received news of the event and passed it to Secretary of State Cordell Hull before Hull met with Japanese Ambasssador Kichisaburo Nomura. The following day, President Roosevelt addressed Congress, giving a speech in which he used the phrase "a date which will live in infamy" and requesting a declaration of war from Congress.

* * *

During the second wave of Japanese air attacks, three bombs hit the destroyer USS *Shaw,* helpless in drydock, and set her magazines off in a massive explosion. In the foreground is the battleship USS *Nevada,* deliberately run aground after her abortive attempt to escape the harbor.

(National Archives photo)

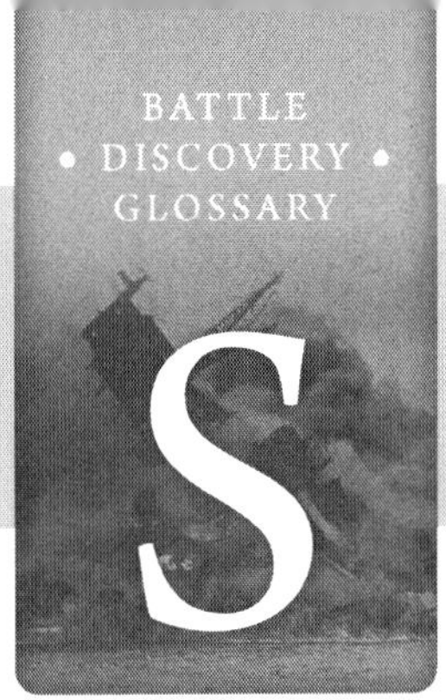

Sacramento (PG-19)

The USS *Sacramento* was a patrol gunboat and the lead in its class when commissioned in April 1914. The gunboat was moored port side to berth B-6, Navy Yard with *Mugford* and *Jarvis* moored alongside to starboard. *Sacramento* was undamaged in the attack and returned fire against Japanese aircraft and also assisted in rescuing sailors from the battleship *Oklahoma. Sacramento* served in Hawaiian waters and near Palmyra Island throughout the war and was decommissioned in February 1946.

Sakamaki, Kazuo (1918–1999)

Ensign Sakamaki became American Prisoner-of-War Number 1 when his two-man midget submarine carrying himself and Kyoshi Inagaki was depth charged and foundered near Waimanalo Beach. However the submarine, *Ha-19,* did not sink but was captured and subsequently taken on tours across American and used in encouraging Americans to buy war bonds.

St. Louis (CL-49)

The light cruiser USS *St. Louis* was the lead in its class and commissioned in May 1939. The ship was moored outboard of *Honolulu* at berth B-21, Navy Yard. *St. Louis* returned fire against attacking aircraft and is credited with downing 3 before getting underway. While in South Channel approaching the open sea *St. Louis* was fired upon by a midget submarine but the torpedo missed. *St. Louis* continued to open sea and patrolled with *Detroit* and *Phoenix* and several destroyers in search of the attacking Japanese fleet. The ship served throughout the war and was decommissioned in June 1946.

Saratoga (CV-3)

The *Lexington*-class aircraft carrier USS *Saratoga* was commissioned in November 1927. The Japanese had hoped *Saratoga* would be in port with *Enterprise* and *Lexington* on the day of the attack, but it was instead entering San Diego Harbor to embark an air group.

San Francisco (CA-38)

The USS *San Franciso* was a *New Orleans*-class heavy cruiser commissioned in February 1934. *San Francisco was*undergoing overhaul at Pearl Harbor Navy Yard berth B-17, and was undamaged in the attack. *San Francisco* served throughout the Pacific Theater and was decommissioned in February 1946.

SBD "Dauntless"

See Douglas SBD "Dauntless."

Schley (DD-103)

The *Wickes*-class destroyer USS *Schley* was commissioned in September1918 and moored alongside *Ramapo* in a nest of ships undergoing overhaul in berth B-20. Undamaged, *Schley* was redesignated as APD-14 effective February 1943 and served in the Pacific throughout the war. In May 1945 the ship was reverted to DD-103 and was decommissioned in November 1945.

SCR-270 radar

Signal Corps Radio model 270 was one of the early-warning radar systems and was used as the U.S. Army's primary long-distance radar throughout the war. It was the model that was being used by Army privates George Elliot and Joe Lockhard at the Opana Mobile Radar Site on the morning of the attack. Elliot and Lockhard detected a large echo on the radar's oscilloscope at 0702 that indicated approaching attack aircraft and reported it to the Aircraft Warning Information Center at Fort Shafter but the contact was mistakenly thought to be incoming B-17 aircraft from California.

Schofield Barracks,

Schofield Barracks was a U.S. Army installation in the middle of Oahu that was close to Wheeler Field. It was established in 1908 and at the time of the attack was the home of the 25th Infantry Division. It was not a target of the Japanese but received strafing.

Second Carrier Division (Japanese)

The Second Carrier Division was an aircraft carrier unit of the Imperial Japanese Navy. During the attack on Pearl Harbor it consisted of the carriers *Sōryū* and *Hiryū* and was commanded by Rear Admiral Yamaguchi Tamon.

Second Submarine Group (Japanese)

The Japanese Second Submarine Group was comprised of *I-1, I-2, I-3, I-4, I-5, I-6,* and *I-7* under the command of Rear Admiral Yamazaki Shigeaki.

Second Wave (Japanese)

Also called Second Attack Wave, the Second Wave was the second of two planned air attacks on U.S. forces at Pearl Harbor and on Oahu. The Second Wave was comprised of 171 aircraft launched from 6 IJN carriers north of Oahu (*Akagi, Kaga, Sōryū, Hiryū, Shōkaku, Zuikaku*). Four planes failed to launch due to mechanical difficulties. Led by Lieutenant Commander Shigekazu Shimazaki, there were 3 groups: the 1st Group targets were Hickam Field, Kaneohe Naval Air Station, Barber's Point, and Pearl Harbor Naval Air Station (Ford Island) and consisted of 54 Nakajima B5N2 "Kates;" the 2nd group targets were battleships and consisted of 78 "Vals"; the 3rd group consisted 36 Mitsubishi A6M2 "Zero" fighters with primary targets of Hickam Field, Bellows Field, Wheeler Field, Kaneohe Naval Air Station, Barber's Point, and Pearl Harbor Naval Air Station (Ford Island). They struck at 0905 and the attack ended at 0945. In the First Wave the "Kates" attacked the ships and the "Vals" attacked the land bases but in the Second Wave the roles were reversed. Twenty aircraft were lost in the Second Wave.

Second Wave First Group (Japanese)
Also listed sometimes as 1st Group, this group consisted of Nakajima "Kate" bombers with armor-piercing bombs, and 54 B5N2 Nakajima "Kates". Its targets were Hickam Field, Kaneohe Naval Air Station, Barber's Point, and Pearl Harbor Naval Air Station (Ford Island).

Second Wave Second Group (Japanese)
Also listed sometimes as 2nd Group, this group consisted of 78 Aichi D3A "Vals" and targets were battleships.

Second Wave Third Group (Japanese)
Also sometimes listed as 3rd Group, this group consisted of 36 Mitsubishi A6M2 "Zero" fighters with primary targets of Hickam Field, Bellows Field, Wheeler Field, Kaneohe Naval Air Station, Barber's Point, and Pearl Harbor Naval Air Station (Ford Island).

***Selfridge* (DD-357)**
The USS *Selfridge* was a *Porter*-class destroyer commissioned in November 1936 and nested with *Conyngham*, *Tucker*, *Case* and *Reid*, undergoing repairs alongside *Whitney* at berth X-0. The ship returned machine gun fire against attacking aircraft

and was undamaged. *Selfridge* continued to serve in the Pacific Theater and was decommissioned in October 1945.

Shaw (DD-373)

The USS *Shaw* was a *Mahan*-class destroyer and sister ship to *Reid*. *Shaw* was commissioned in September 1936 and dry-docked at YFD-2 and hit by three bombs. Fires spread quickly throughout the ship and it was heavily damaged from the bombs, fires, and the forward magazine that exploded about 0930. *Shaw* was repaired, returned to service in June 1942, and continued to serve throughout the war before being decommissioned in October 1945.

Shimezaki, Shigekazu (1908–1945)

Lieutenant Commander Shimezaki was flying a Nakajima B5N2 "Kate" and was commander of the Second Wave. He was killed in action near Taiwan while serving as a staff officer of the IJN 3rd Air Fleet on January 9, 1945.

Shinkoku Maru

The Japanese tanker was part of Supply Group One. It was sunk by U.S. Navy aircraft at Truk on February 17, 1944.

Shiranui

The *Shiranui* ("Unknown Fire) was a *Kagerō*-class Japanese destroyer that served as part of the attack force. The ship was later sunk by aircraft of Task Force 77 on October 27, 1944, 80 miles north of the Philippine island Panay.

Shōkaku

Shōkaku ("Flying Crane"), was 1 of 6 Japanese carriers that participated in the attack (*Akagi*, *Kaga*, *Hiryū*, *Shōkaku*, *Sōryū*, *Zuikaku*). The carrier was sunk on June 19, 1944 by 3 torpedoes from USS *Cavalla* (SS-244) 140 miles north of Yap Island in the Caroline Islands.

Short, Walter C. (1880–1949)

Lieutenant-General Short was Commander, Hawaiian Department of the U.S. Army. Along with Admiral Kimmel, he was responsible for American forces in the Hawaiian Islands. He was comfortable with the defense posture of the Army and believed the Navy would protect Hawaii from air attack. His primary concern was attack and espionage by *nisei*—American born Japanese in Hawaii, of which there about 100,000. On 27 November 1941, Short received a war warning order from Chief of Staff General George C. Marshall but responded with limited action. He was relieved of command on December 16, 1941, reduced in rank to Major General, and allowed to retire.

Sicard (DM-21)

Originally commissioned in June 1920 as a *Clemson*-class destroyer, USS *Sicard* was later converted to a high-speed minelayer. *Sicard* was moored starboard side to *Pruitt* in berth B-18 at the Navy Yard undergoing overhaul and was undamaged. She served in the Pacific throughout the war and was decommissioned in November 1945.

Solace AH-5

The USS *Solace* was built in 1927 as the passenger ship SS *Iroquois* and later acquired by the Navy and converted to a hospital ship and commissioned August 1941. *Solace* was moored at berth X-4 and moved to berth X-13 at 0900. She was undamaged in the attack and sent motor launches with stretcher parties to *Arizona* and *West Virginia,* and boat crews to assist *Oklahoma. Solace* served throughout the Pacific during the war and was decommissioned in March 1946.

Sōryū

Sōryū ("Blue Dragon"), was 1 of 6 Japanese carriers that participated in the attack (*Akagi, Kaga, Hiryū, Shōkaku, Sōryū, Zuikaku*). It was attacked by planes from USS *Yorktown* (CV-5) on June 4, 1942 at the Battle of Midway with assistance from a torpedo from USS *Nautilus* (SS-168) shortly after the aircraft attack.

Sotoyomo (YT-9)

The USS *Sotoyomo* was a harbor tug and lead in its class launched in 1903. *Sotoyomo* was burned and sunk by explosions and fires from *Shaw* but was repaired and placed back in service in August 1942, serving in the South Pacific until being scuttled off Leyte Island in February 1946.

Southeast Loch

See Pearl Harbor.

Special Attack Unit

The Special Attack Unit was the group of 5 submarines (*I-16, I-18, I-20, I-22, I-24*) that carried the 5 midget submarines that attacked Pearl Harbor. It was commanded by Captain Hanku Sasaki.

Submarine Squadron 1 (Japanese)

See First Submarine Squadron.

Submarine Squadron 2 (Japanese)

See Second Submarine Squadron.

Submarine Squadron 3 (Japanese)

See Third Submarine Squadron.

***Sumner* (AG-32)**

The USS *Sumner* was a miscellaneous auxiliary and later a survey ship (AGS-5) originally commissioned in November 1915 as submarine tender USS *Bushnell* (AS-2). *Sumner* was moored to the new dock at the southern end of the Submarine Base, bow to eastward alongside *Castor* and sustained minor injuries to gun crews incurred while firing on aircraft. *Sumner* served throughout the Pacific and was decommissioned in September 1946.

***Sunnadin* (AT-28)**

The USS *Sunnadin* was an ocean-going tug commissioned October 1919, and decommissioned April 1946.

Swan (AVP-7)

The seaplane tender USS *Swan* was originally commissioned in January 1919 as a *Lapwing*-class minesweeper (AM-34) but redesignated in January 1936 and serving as tender for Patrol Wing Two. On the day of the attack, *Swan* was resting on the marine railway dock, in boiler upkeep. *Swan* returned fire against aircraft with her 3-inch anti-aircraft guns and was undamaged. *Swan* served throughout the war and was decommissioned in December 1945.

Nakajima B5N2 "Kate" leaves the *Shōkaku* for Pearl Harbor.

(U.S. Navy, National archives Photo # 80-G-182249)

* * *

The remains of a P-40 "Tomahawk" at Wheeler Field being cannibalized for parts to get other salvageable aircraft into the air.

(National Archives photo)

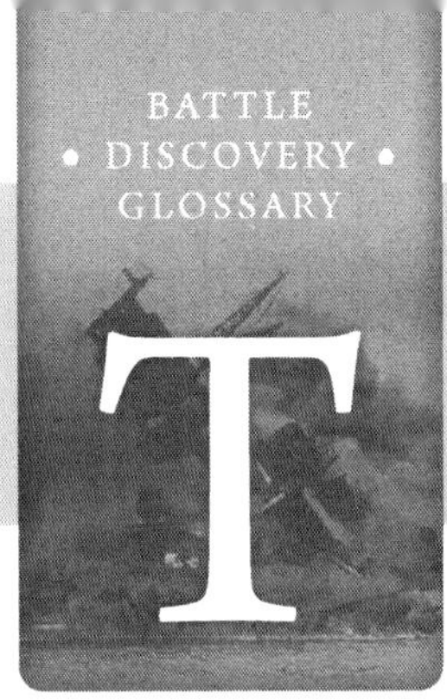

Taiyo Maru

The Japanese merchant ship *Taiyo Maru* came to Pearl Harbor on November 1, 1941, ostensibly to pick up any Japanese citizens that wanted to depart due to the collapse of trade talks with the United States. However, the ship carried 3 Japanese naval officers who were collecting intelligence for submarines and other aspects of the coming attack, including intelligence from the principle espionage agent ashore, Ensign Takeo Yoshikawa, who provided written responses to intelligence questions sent from the ship.

Takakashi, Kakuichi (1904–1942)

Lieutenant Commander Takakashi commanded the First Wave of dive-bombers and 15th Attack Unit of "Vals" from the carrier *Shōkaku.* Takakashi received the signal to attack from Lieutenant Commder Mitsuo Fuchida, who fired a flare as the final confirmation that the Japanese had not been detected and were to continue with the surprise attack. His air group struck the PBY ramp at Ford Island at 0755 and opened the attack.

Taney (WHEC-37)

The U.S. Coast Guard high-endurance cutter USCG *Taney* was commissioned in October 1936. On July 25, 1941, *Taney* was transferred to the Navy and reported for duty with the local defense forces of the 14th Naval District (Destroyer Division 80). She was moored alongside Pier 6 in Honolulu Harbor at the time of the attack. *Taney* was undamaged in the attack and continued to serve in the Pacific and Atlantic Theaters throughout the war. *Taney* was decommissioned in December 1986.

Tangier (AV-8)

The USS *Tangier* was a seaplane tender that was originally a cargo ship and commissioned in September 1941. *Tangier* was berthed at F-10, Ford Island, with *Utah* moored at F-11 directly astern and *Raleigh* at F-12. *Tangier* sustained minor damage by several bomb near-misses. *Tangier* served throughout the war in the Pacific Theater and was decommissioned in January 1947.

Tanikaze

The *Kagerō*-class Japanese destroyer *Tanikaze* ("Valley Wind") was commissioned in April 1941 and served as part of the escort for the Japanese carriers and attack force. *Tanikaze* was torpedoed and sunk by USS *Harder* (SS-257) 90 miles southwest of Basilan, June 9, 1944.

Tankan Bay

See Hitokappu Bay.

Taussig, Joseph K. Jr. (1920–1999)
Ensign Taussig was Officer of the Deck aboard *Nevada* at the time of the attack and responsible in part for getting the ship underway.

***Tautog* (SS-199)**
The USS *Tautog* was a *Tambor*-class submarine commissioned in July 1940 and moored in Southeast Loch at pier two alongside *Dolphin* near the Merry Point Landing at the submarine base. Undamaged in the attack, *Tautog*'s gun crew assisted in downing 1 aircraft. *Tautog* served throughout the war and was decommissioned in December 1945.

***Tennessee* (BB-43)**
The USS *Tennessee* was the lead battleship in its class and was commissioned in June 1920. *Tennessee* was on Battleship Row moored starboard side to mooring quay F-6, next to *West Virginia* and forward of *Arizona*. She received relatively minor damage, was repaired by February 1942, and served throughout the war in the Aleutians Islands Campaign and in the Pacific. *Tennessee* was decommissioned in February 1947.

***Tern* (AM-31)**
The USS *Tern* was a *Lapwing*-class minesweeper commissioned in May 1931. On December 7th, *Tern* was on the north end of 1010 dock undergoing upkeep alongside *Argonne*. Undamaged in the attack, *Tern* was underway at 0943 and assisted in picking up survivors from *Arizona* and fighting fires

of *West Virginia. Tern* served throughout the Pacific during the war and was decommissioned in December 1945.

Ten Ten Dock

Dock 1010, also known as 1010 Dock, was a long drydock pier at the Navy Yard named for the longest ship it could hold—1010 feet. During the attack, it was occupied by *Helena* and *Oglala.*

Thomas, Francis J. (1904–2005)

Lieutenant Commander (later, Rear Admiral) Thomas was ranking officer aboard *Nevada* at the time of the attack and responsible for getting the ship underway along with officer of the deck Ensign Joseph K. Taussig, Jr.

Third Submarine Group (Japanese)

This group was comprised of *I-8, I-68, I-69, I-70, I-71, I-72, I-73, I-74,* and *I-75* and was commanded by Rear Admiral Miwa Shigeyoshi.

Third Wave (Japanese)

Also called Third Attack Wave, the Third Wave refers to the possibility and counterfactual of a third strike by Japanese aircraft specifically targeting land-based installations, repair facilities, and fuel storage facilities. Admiral Nagumo's decision not to risk the carriers or planes in a third wave attack left repair capabilities and fuel stores of 4.5 million barrels of oil undamaged. Many have argued that had they been destroyed, the Pacific Fleet would have had to return to the west coast of the U.S. for homeporting and the ability to begin a counter-offensive would have been significantly delayed.

Thornton (AVD-11)

The USS *Thornton* was originally a *Clemson*-class destroyer (DD-270) commissioned in July 1919, and in June 1940, recommissioned, converted, and reclassified a seaplane tender. *Thornton* was moored port side to dock at berth S-1 in Southeast Loch at the submarine base and undamaged. *Thornton* served until decommissioning in May 1945 following an April 1945 collision with USS *Ashtabula* (AO-51) and USS *Escalante* (AO-70).

Thresher (SS-200)

The *Tambor*-class submarine USS *Thresher* was commissioned in August 1940. At the time of the attack, *Thresher* was returning to Pearl Harbor under the escort of *Litchfield* (DD-336). Upon notification of the Japanese attack, *Litchfield* departed to join other forces searching for the Japanese. *Thresher* began its own patrol and upon later attempting to safely return to homeport and enter the harbor, *Thresher* was initially driven away by mistaken attacks, postponing its return until 8 December, when she was escorted in by *Thornton*. *Thresher* served throughout the war making 15 patrols and was decommissioned in December 1945. Recommissioned in February 1946 with the intent of being used as a target ship at Bikini Atoll, *Thresher* was decommissioned a final time in July 1946 after it was decided that is was not economically feasible to use the boat.

Tiger (WSC-152)

The U.S. Coast Guard *Active*-class patrol boat *Tiger* was commissioned in 1927 and on patrol off Barbers Point at the time of the attack and came under fire from an aircraft but was undamaged. *Tiger* was one of the first vessels to fire on the Japanese aircraft. *Tiger* was decommissioned in 1948.

Toei Maru

The *Toei Maru* was an IJN oiler that was part of Supply Group 2. It was later sunk by USS *Silversides* (SS-236), January 18, 1943.

Tohu Maru

The *Tohu Maru* was an IJN tanker and flagship of Supply Group 2. It was later sunk by USS *Gudgeon* (SS-211) on March 29, 1943.

Tojo, Hideki (1884–1948)

Hideki Tojo was a General in the Imperial Japanese Army as well as Prime Minister of Japan. He was previously Minister of War and retained that position as well as Chief of Staff of the Army (and others), thus giving him enormous power and control over plans and decisions for war. He resigned after the fall of Saipan in July 1944 and after the defeat of Japan, he was tried as a war criminal, found guilty, and hanged.

Tone

The Japanese heavy cruiser *Tone* was named for the Tone River. It was the lead ship in the *Tone*-class and was commissioned in November 1938. *Tone* was designed for long-range scouting and had the capacity for 6 seaplanes for reconnaissance. Along with sister ship *Tone,* the mission on December 7th was to provide weather reconnaissance and picket patrol and launched 1 Aichi 13A1 Type 0 "Jake" floatplane and 1 Nakajima E8N Type 95 "Dave" floatplane (*Tone* did the same, *Hiei* and *Kirishima* also launched floatplanes for patrol). *Tone* was sunk during the large bombing raid of Kure in July 1945.

"To, to, to,"

"*To, to, to*" was the coded signal that was short for "Totsugeki seyo!" meaning "Charge!" that was ordered at 0749 by Mitsuo Fuchida, leader of the First Wave, to Petty Officer 1st Class Norinobu Mizuki to send to other attacking aircraft.

"Tora, Tora, Tora"

"*Tora, Tora, Tora*" ("Tiger, Tiger, Tiger"), was the Japanese codeword used to indicate that complete surprise had been achieved. It was sent by Mitsuo Fuchida to the *Akagi* to be relayed back to Tokyo.

Torpedoes (Japanese)

Torpedoes as an aerial weapon had proved viable to use in the British attack on ships in the Italian port of Taranto in November 1940 where 3 Italian battleships, *Littorio*, *Duilo* and

Cavour were struck. The attack was closely studied by Admiral Yamamoto's staff as they planned the "Hawaii Operation." One difficulty the Japanese had to overcome was the shallow depth of Pearl Harbor. This required modifying the Japanese Type 91 Model II torpedoes that would be dropped from the Nakajima B5N2 "Kate" bombers. To do so, wooden fins were added that gave more stability and buoyancy to the torpedoes and reduced their running depth from about 65 feet to 40 feet. They had a 205-kg (452 lb) warhead and most of the ships sunk in the attack were sunk by these torpedoes.

Tracy (DM-19)

The USS *Tracy* was commissioned as a *Clemson*-class destroyer (DD-214) in March 1920 and reclassified as a high-speed minesweeper in June 1937. *Tracy* was moored portside to berth B-15, Navy Yard, unarmed, disabled, undergoing overhaul. *Preble* and *Cummings* were moored to starboard in that order. Undamaged in the attack, *Tracy* continued to serve in the Pacific Theater throughout the war and was decommissioned in January 1946.

Trever (DMS-16)

The USS *Terver* was commissioned as a *Clemson*-class destroyer (DD-339) in August 1922 and reclassified as a high-speed minesweeper in November 1940. *Trever* was moored in West Loch at buoy D-7 along with *Wasmuth*, *Zane*, and *Perry*. *Trever* was undamaged in the attack and continued service in the Pacific Theater until the war's end. She was decommissioned in November 1945.

Tucker (DD-374)

The *Mahan*-class destroyer USS *Tucker* was commissioned in July 1936 and moored in East Loch with *Whitney*, *Reid*, *Conyngham*, *Case*, and *Selfridge* at berth X-8. *Tucker* was undamaged in the attack and returned fire on enemy aircraft claiming the downing of 3 airplanes. In August 1942, *Tucker* struck a mine off Espiritu Santo and sank.

Turkey (AM-13)

The USS *Turkey* was a *Lapwing*-class minesweeper commissioned in December 1918. She was moored in a nest at the Coal Dock with *Rail*, *Bobolink*, and *Vireo*. Undamaged in the attack, *Turkey* served in the Pacific Theater until the war's end and was decommissioned in December 1946.

Two-Ocean Navy Act

Also known as the Vinson-Walsh Act, the Two-Ocean Navy Act was a U.S. law passed in the House of Representatives 316–0 on July 19, 1940. The act authorized acquisition of ships and aircraft for the Navy with the result of increasing its size by 70% at a cost of $8.55 billion. On June 17, 1940, Admiral Harold R. Stark, the Chief of Naval Operations, against the backdrop of the expanding war in Europe, of which the U.S. was not yet a belligerent, requested the funds to build a "two-ocean Navy." Approved and signed by President Roosevelt, the act included, but was not limited to: 7 battleships, 6 battlecruisers, 18 carriers, 27 cruisers, 115 destroyers, and 43 submarines), production of 15,000 aircraft, conversion of auxiliary ships, and construction and renovation of facilities. It was viewed at the time as an attempt to deter any Japanese or German attack on the United States. Many of the ships came online in 1943, significantly boosting U.S. naval capabilities.

Tyler, Kermit A. (1913–2010)
Kermit Tyler was a U.S. Army Air Corps officer serving as Executive Officer of the 78th Pursuit Squadron. On the day of the attack he was on duty as Officer in Charge of the radar information center at Fort Shafter that received a phone call from Opana Point reporting a radar contact representing incoming aircraft. Untrained and new on the job, Tyler told Privates Elliot and Lockard, "Don't worry about it" assuming it to be the scheduled flight of 6 incoming B-17s from California. In August 1942, a Naval Board of Inquiry found that he had been assigned to the information center without proper training, supervision, or personnel and he was cleared of any wrongdoing. He retired from the U.S. Air Force as a Lieutenant Colonel in 1961.

Type 97 60-kg land bomb (Japanese)
was a 132-lb bomb carried by the Nakijima B5N2 "Kates" during the Second Wave and used against ground targets.

Type 98 250-kg land bomb (Japanese)
The Type 98 was a 551-lb bomb carried by the Aichi D3A1 "Vals" in the First Wave and the Nakijima B5N2 "Kates" during the Second Wave and used against ground targets.

Type 99 Model 1 250-kg bomb (Japanese)
The Type 99 was a 551-lb anti-ship bomb carried by the Aichi D3A1 "Vals" of the Second Wave.

Type 99 Model 5 800-kg bomb (Japanese)
The Type 99 was a 1760-lb armor-piercing bomb that was carried by the 49 Nakijima B5N2 "Kate" aircraft during the First Wave. It was one of these converted 16-inch naval shells that caused the final explosion sinking *Arizona.*

Type 91 Model 2 250-kg aerial torpedo (Japanese)
See Torpedoes.

* * *

The USS *Utah* (AG 16) capsizing after the Japanese attack on Pearl Harbor. The battleship turned target ship was one of the three U.S. Navy battleships irretrievably lost during the attack.

(U.S. Naval History and Heritage Command photo)

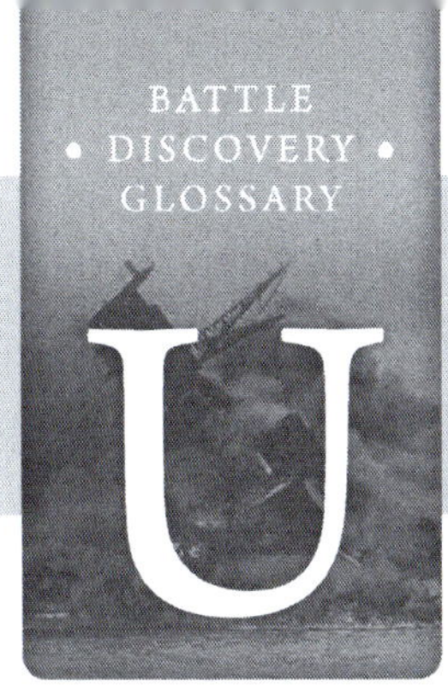

Ugaki, Matome (1890–1945)
Rear Admiral (later, Vice Admiral) Ugaki was Chief of Staff to Admiral Isoroku Yamamoto. He is also known for his kamikaze attack and death several hours after learning of Japan's defeat on August 15, 1945.

U.S. Coast Guard
U.S. Coast Guard ships and personnel were active during the attack. Coast Guard vessels in service in Hawaii included the 327-foot cutter *Taney*, the 190-foot buoy tender *Kukui*, two 125-foot patrol craft: *Reliance* and *Tiger*, and several smaller craft. At the time of the attack, *Taney* was tied up at Pier 6 in Honolulu Harbor, *Reliance* and the unarmed *Kukui* both lay at Pier 4 and *Tiger* was on patrol along the western shore of Oahu. At the Barbers Point Light Station, Keeper John L. Sweeney, also witnessed the attack and filed an after-action report of it.

U.S. Marine Corps,
U.S Marine Corps personnel numbered about 4,500 at Pearl Harbor and in the area including the Marine Barracks at the

Pearl Harbor Navy Yard and Marine Air Group 21 (MAG-21) at Marine Corps Air Station at Ewa, Oahu. MAG-21 lost nearly all of its 47 aircraft in the First Wave. The latter was the first target struck about 2 minutes before the ships at Pearl Harbor were attacked. There were more than 800 Marines serving aboard ships at Pearl Harbor with detachments aboard USS *Arizona*, *California*, *Helena*, *Honolulu*, *Maryland*, *Nevada*, *Oklahoma*, *Pennsylvania*, *Tennessee*, *Utah*, and *West Virgina*. *Arizona* had the largest loss of Marines with only 15 of 82 surviving. In total, there were 112 Marines killed and missing in action and more than 64 wounded. Other Marine units on Oahu included: 2d Engineer Battalion, 2d Service Battalion, 1st Defense Battalion 9 (rear echelon), 3d Defense Battalion, 4th Defense Battalion, and a few Marines from the 6th Defense Battalion.

U.S. Pacific Fleet

The U.S. Pacific Fleet was created originally in 1907 and recreated in February 1941 with the United States Fleet being split into the Atlantic Fleet, the Pacific Fleet, and the Asiatic Fleet. The Pacific Fleet base had changed its homeport from San Diego, California to Pearl Harbor in May 1940. There were 207 ships total in the Pacific Fleet and 103 ships (185 vessels total) in Pearl Harbor on December 7, 1941.

Urakaze

The *Kagerō*-class destroyer *Urakaze* ("Wind on the Sea") was commissioned in December 1940 that sailed as an escort for the attacking aircraft carriers. *Urakaze* was torpedoed and sunk by USS *Sealion* (SS-315) on November 21, 1944.

Uritsky

The *Uritsky* was a Soviet freighter that was in the same area as the Japanese attacking force and may have crossed its path on December 5th, although this is uncertain and there was no report by the *Uritsky* of the force (something that would have been the captain's decision).

Utah (AG-16)

Utah was a miscellaneous auxiliary vessel and ex-battleship (target/AA training ship) moored at mooring quay F-11 off Ford Island, between *Raleigh* forward and *Tangier* astern; hit by two torpedoes and capsized. It was the first ship hit in the attack, a total loss, and had 64 dead. Based on intelligence regarding its status, Japanese torpedo planes had been told not to waste bombs attacking the ship however 6 of 8 *Sōryū* torpedo bombers did so. The first torpedo hit at 0801 and by 0812 *Utah* had rolled onto her port side. Declared to be "in ordinary" on December 29, *Utah* was eventually partly righted but difficulties arose and further attempts were abandoned and the ship was placed out of commission in September 1944. *Utah* joins *Arizona* and *Oklahoma* as the three ships that did not return to service after the attack. Crewmembers who died when *Utah* sank were never removed and the ship remains a war grave. *Utah* was originally a *Florida*-class dreadnought battleship commissioned in August 1911 and had seen service during the 1914 Mexican Revolution and the First World War. Under the terms of the London Naval Treaty of 1930, *Utah* was reclassified as a radio-controlled target ship, redesignated AG-16, and recommissioned in 1932.

Imperial Japanese Navy destroyer *Urakaze* (1940)

(Public Domain)

* * *

A Japanese Aichi D3A1 "Val" dive bomber, dive brakes and bomb crutch still extended, pulls out of its dive low over Pearl Harbor.

(U.S. Navy History and Heritage Command photo)

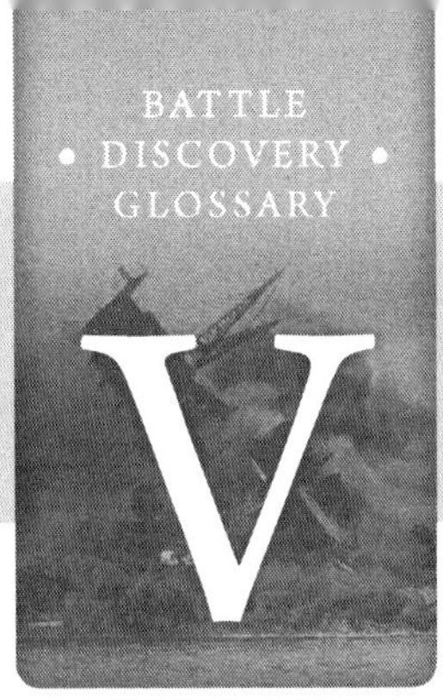

"Val"

See Aichi D3A.

***Vestal* (AR-4)**

The USS *Vestal* was a repair ship that was originally built as a fleet collier with a civilian crew but refitted and commissioned in September 1913 as a repair ship. *Vestal* was moored port side to the port side of the *Arizona* at F-7. She was hit by two bombs, explosion and fire from *Arizona*, and beached. After repairs and alterations *Vesta*l returned to service in August 1942, served throughout the Pacific Theater, and was decommissioned in August 1946.

***Vireo* (AM-52)**

The USS *Vireo* was a *Lawing*-class minesweeper commissioned in October 1919 moored inboard at the Coal Dock with *Turkey*, *Bobolink*, and *Rail* moored outboard. *Viero* was undamaged in the attack and assisted the battleship *California*. She served throughout the war and was decommissioned in April 1946.

Vought OS2U

The Vought OS2U "Kingfisher" was a catapult-launched observation floatplane on battleships, heavy cruisers, and light cruisers. There were several aboard ships and ashore that were destroyed in the attack.

VP

See Patrol Wing One and Patrol Wing Two.

USS *Vestal* beached and listing

(U.S. Navy photo #80-G-19933, National Archives)

* * *

Rescuing survivors near the USS *West Virginia*

(80-G-19930)

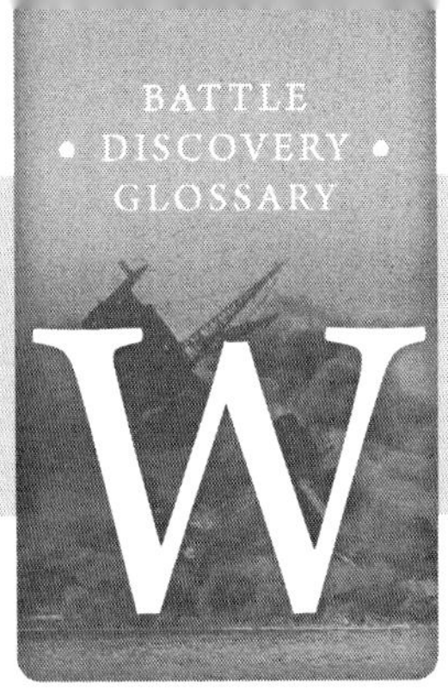

War Plan Orange

War Plan Orange was the designation for a series of war plans produced by the United States Joint Army and Navy Board between 1919 and 1938 dealing with a potential war with Japan. The plan originally assumed that the United States would be fighting without allies, but by 1941, the plan was subsumed into the larger Rainbow series of war plans that broadened the scenarios.

Ward (DD-139)

The USS *Ward* was a *Wickes*-class destroyer originally commissioned in July 1918. Decommissioned in 1921, *Ward* was recommissioned in January 1941 and on December 7th was patrolling the entrance to Pearl Harbor. At 0637, she attacked and sank midget submarine *No. 20,* firing the first American shots of the war. The commanding officer, Commander William W. Outerbridge had taken command the day before the attack. *Ward* was undamaged in the Pearl Harbor attack and continued to serve until being struck by a kamikaze attack on December 7, 1944 resulting in uncontrolled fires, the order to abandon ship, and subsequent sinking by gunfire from *O'Brien.* Interestingly, Commander Outerbridge was commanding officer of the *O'Brien* when it brought *Ward* to its end.

Wasmuth (DMS-15)

Wasmuth was originally a *Clemson*-class destroyer (DD-338) commissioned in December 1921 and reclassified as a high speed minelayer in November 1940. *Wasmuth* was moored in a nest with Mine Division Four at buoys D-7 and D-7s; order from port to starboard: *Trever*, *Wasmuth*, *Zane*, and *Perry*. Undamaged in the attack, the ship is credited with shooting down 1 airplane that crashed on Waipio Peninsula near Middle Loch. *Wasmuth* sank on 29 December 1942 while escorting a convoy through a heavy Alaskan storm.

West Loch

See Pearl Harbor.

West Virginia (BB-48)

The battleship *West Virginia* was the youngest battleship at Pearl Harbor and a *Colorado*-class battleship commissioned in December 1923. *West Virginia* was moored on Battleship Row outboard of *Tennessee* at mooring quay F-6, forward of *Arizona.* She was hit by several aerial torpedoes and bombs and began flooding and listing more than 20 degrees. Counter-flooding was performed by the crew and the ship sunk but settled upright on the bottom of the harbor. The ship was floated, and rebuilt by July 1944. Many sailors were trapped in *West Virginia* and 67 died. *West Virginia* was in Tokyo Bay at surrender of the Japanese on 24 August 1945. She was decommissioned in January 1947.

Wheeler Field

Wheeler Field was the main U.S. Army Air Corps base on Oahu with and headquarters for the 14th Pursuit Wing, 15th Pursuit Group, and 18th Pursuit Group, totaling about 145 aircraft of which 42 were destroyed and 56 damaged and out of service in the two attack waves. Wheeler Field was a primary target. Several American aircraft did get airborne and fought against the Japanese scoring the first American aerial victories of the war. There were 33 fatalities and 77 wounded at Wheeler Field.

***Whitney* (AD-4)**

The USS *Whitney* was a *Dobbin*-class destroyer tender commissioned in September 1924. She was moored bow and stern to buoys X-8 and X-8S with *Conyngham*, *Reid*, *Tucker*, *Case*, and *Selfridge* moored alongside to port. *Whitney* was undamaged and continued service until being decommissioned in October 1946.

***Widgeon* (ASR-1)**

The USS *Widgeon* was originally a *Lapwing*-class minesweeper (AM-22) commissioned in July 1918 and reclassified in January 1936 as a submarine rescue ship. She was berthed at the Submarine Base and undamaged in the attack. *Widgeon* assisted in salvage operations of *California, Nevada,* and *Oklahoma* and continued service until decommissioning in February 1947.

Worden (DD-352)

The *Farragut*-class destroyer *Worden* was commissioned in January 1935. She was alongside destroyer tender *Dobbin* receiving maintenance at berth X-2 off the northeastern shore of Ford Island, nested with *Hull, Phelps, Dewey,* and *MacDonough. Worden* received no damage, returned fire and is credited with downing 1 aircraft, and got underway within 2 hours. *Worden* served in the Pacific until being sunk by a hull breach in the rock-edged harbor of Constantine Harbor in the Aleutian Islands on January 12, 1943.

Destroyed Army aircraft at Wheeler Field after the attack (Photo SC #134-872, National Archives)

* * *

Isoroku Yamamoto

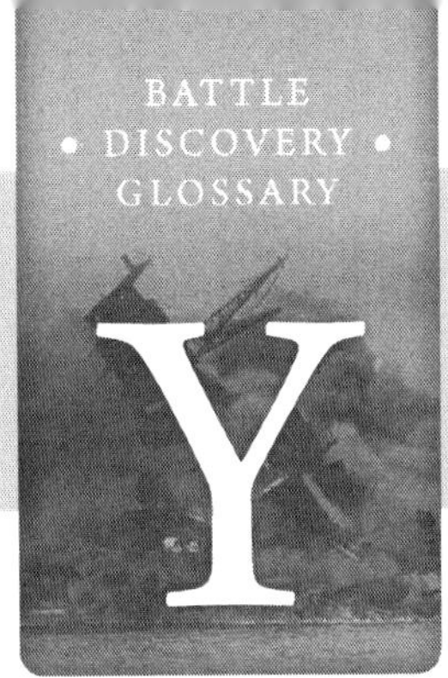

Yamamoto, Isoroku (1884–1943)
Admiral Yamamoto was Commander, Combined Fleet of the Imperial Japanese Navy. He opposed war with the United States, but when it became inevitable from the Japanese perspective, he oversaw the planning of the attack on Pearl Harbor. In June 1942, he led the Combined Fleet at the Battle of Midway, where he lost 4 aircraft carriers. In April 1943, the U.S. learned he would be flying to the Solomon Islands for an inspection and U.S. Army Air Corps assets from the 339th Fighter Squadron, 347th Fighter Group attacked and shot down his plane in what was called "Operation Vengeance."

Yoshikawa, Takeo (1914–1993)
Takeo Yoshikawa was Foreign Office chancelor at the Japanese consulate in Honolulu. He was naval officer, part of the Imperial Japanese Navy General Staff and conducted espionage under the name Tadashi Morimura sending detailed reports of U.S. Navy Pacific Fleet activities by means of the JN-19 code. No one knew the U.S. Pacific Fleet better than he and his work was a key to the success of the attack.

• • •

A6M2 "Zero" fighters prepare to launch from *Akagi* as part of the second wave during the attack on Pearl Harbor.

(Photo is from the Makiel Collection via Wenger)

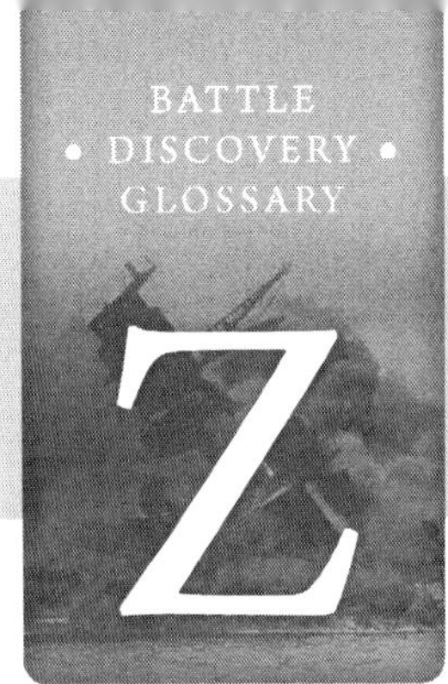

"Z flag"

The "Z flag" was the international maritime signal flag for the letter "Z" and Japanese flag that Admiral Heihachiro Togo (1848–1934) had flown at the 1905 Battle of Tsushima during the Russo-Japanese War. It was raised on Vice-Admiral Nagumo's flagship *Akagi* before aircraft were flown off the carrier to attack Pearl Harbor recalling the victory at Tsushima as well as the early stages of the Pearl Harbor attack plans known as "Operation Z." Interestingly, when hoisted at Tsushima, the flag had the predesignated meaning "The fate of the Empire rests on the outcome of this battle. Let each man do his utmost." This was itself reminiscent of Vice-Admiral Horatio, Lord Nelson's hoisted signal at the Battle of Trafalgar (1805), "England expects every man will do his duty."

***Zane* (DMS-14)**

Originally a *Clemson*-class destroyer (DD-337), the USS *Zane* was commissioned in February 1921 and converted to and reclassified as a high speed minesweeper in November 1940. On December 7th the *Zane* was moored bow and stern in a nest with Mine Division Four at buoys D-7 and D-7s; order from port to starboard: *Trever*, *Wasmuth*, *Zane*, and *Perry*. Undamaged in the attack, Zane returned fire against aircraft and also at 0830, sighted the midget submarine *No. 22* astern of *Medussa.* Unable to fire upon it due to *Zane*'s position, *No. 22* was rammed by *Monaghan. Zane* continued to serve in the Pacific Theater until decommissioning in December 1945.

"Zeke"
See Mitsubishi A6M2 "Zero."

"Zero"
See Mitsubishi A6M2 "Zero."

Zuikaku
The was *Zuikaku* ("Auspicious Crane") was 1 of 6 Japanese carriers that participated in the attack (*Akagi, Kaga, Hiryū, Shōkaku, Sōryū, Zuikaku*). Struck and sunk by torpedoes from aircraft from USS *Essex* (CV-9) and USS *Lexington* (CV-16) on 25 October 1944, 220 miles east northeast of Cape Engano, during the Battle of Leyte Gulf.

Japanese aircraft carrier *Zuikaku* in November 1941 (Public Domain)

• • •

APPENDICES

It's All in a Name: Allied Identification of Japanese Planes

During the attack on Pearl Harbor and the surrounding airfields on Oahu the defenders saw four varieties aircraft being flown by the Japanese attackers. Among the group of planes were fighters, dive bombers, torpedo planes, and horizontal bombers. Most of the eyewitness referred to them as Japanese "Zeros" [*sic*]. It appears that part of that reference of "Zero" was derived from the large red circles on the fuselage and wings of the Japanese aircraft. The red circle was called a "meatball" by some defenders. The challenge of identifying these planes was significant and accuracy was not easy. The Japanese nomenclature of their aircraft was complicated by their system of manufacturers, models, types, and the year the aircraft entered service. The problem was magnified in the early part of the war with both the U.S. Navy and Army having separate Japanese plane identification systems.

Enter the "McCoy System." Captain Frank McCoy, U.S. Army Air Forces, in 1942 coordinated with the 38th

Bombardment and the Allied Technical Intelligence Group a plan to come up with ingenuous system for identifying Japanese aircraft. Two other team members Tech. Sgt. Francis Williams and Cpl. Joseph Grattan took on the task with McCoy in selecting the types of aircraft and how they would be divided. For example, names of boys would be used fighters and girls names to bombers, seaplanes and other multi-engine aircraft. Trainers were named after trees. By early 1943 the allied forces in the Pacific had coded all Japanese aircraft that were flying at that time of the war.

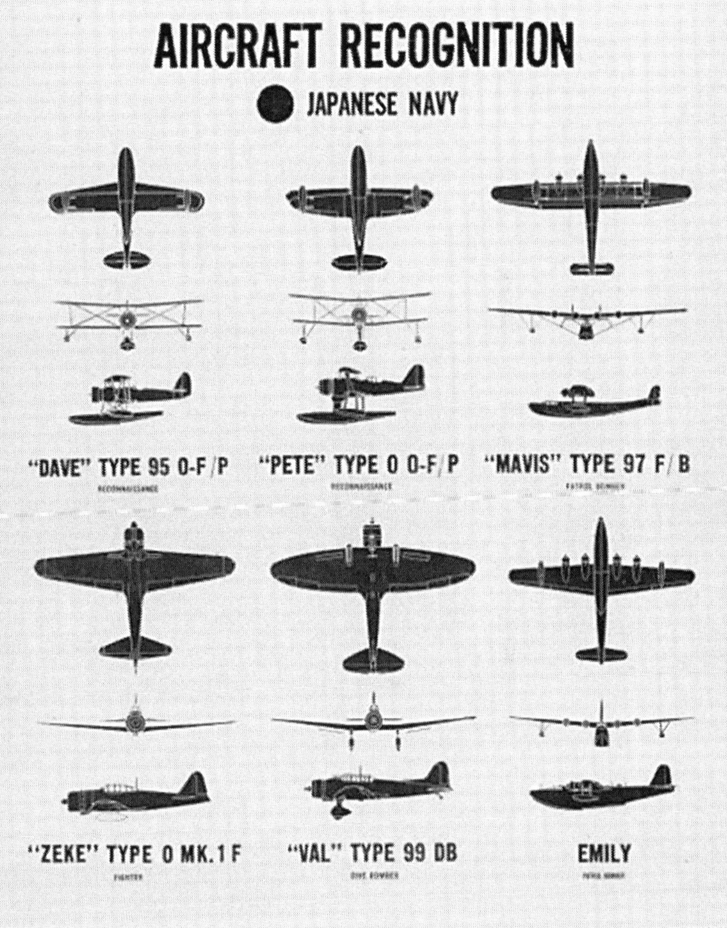
AIRCRAFT RECOGNITION
JAPANESE NAVY
"DAVE" TYPE 95 O-F/P
"PETE" TYPE 0 O-F/P
"MAVIS" TYPE 97 F/B
"ZEKE" TYPE 0 MK.1 F
"VAL" TYPE 99 DB
EMILY
© 2014 BYRD

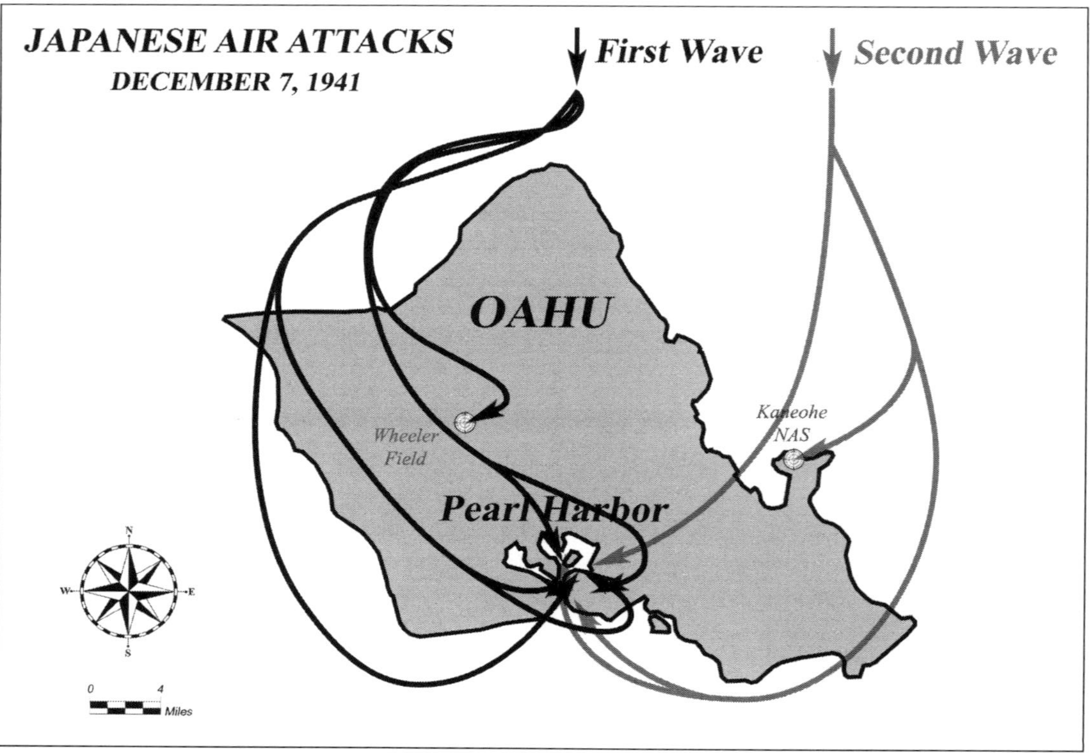
JAPANESE AIR ATTACKS
DECEMBER 7, 1941
First Wave
Second Wave
OAHU
Wheeler Field
Kaneohe NAS
Pearl Harbor
N
W
E
S
0
4
Miles

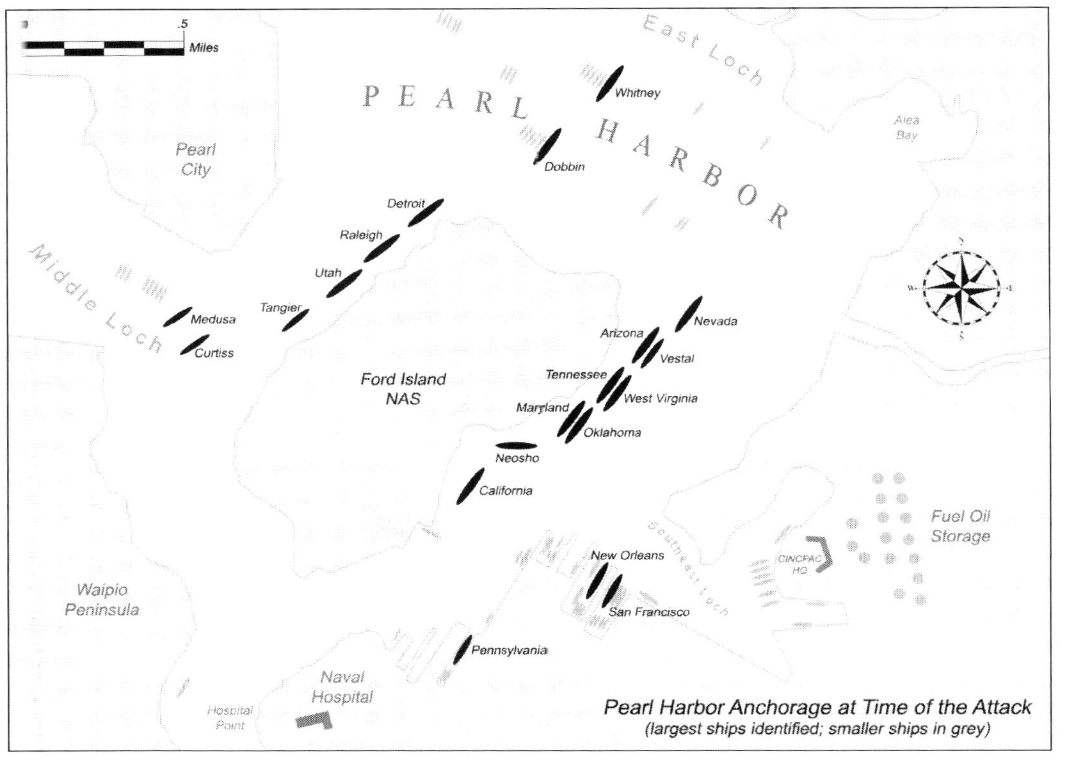
.5
Miles
PEARL HARBOR
East Loch
Middle Loch
Southeast Loch
Aiea Bay
Pearl City
Ford Island NAS
Waipio Peninsula
Naval Hospital
Hospital Point
Fuel Oil Storage
CINCPAC HQ
Whitney
Dobbin
Detroit
Raleigh
Utah
Tangier
Medusa
Curtiss
Nevada
Arizona
Vestal
Tennessee
West Virginia
Maryland
Oklahoma
Neosho
California
New Orleans
San Francisco
Pennsylvania
Pearl Harbor Anchorage at Time of the Attack
(largest ships identified; smaller ships in grey)

RECOMMENDED READING

The few titles listed below are among the many excellent works available on the history of the attack at Pearl Harbor. These are presented for the general reader who wishes to pursue the topic in greater detail.

Cohen, Stan. *Attack on Pearl Harbor: A Pictorial History.* Missoula, MT: Pictorial Histories Publishing Co., Inc., 2001.

Goldstein, Donald M. and Katherine V. Dillon, eds. *The Pearl Harbor Papers.* New York: Brassey's, 1993.

Hoyt, Edwin B. *Yamamoto: The Man Who Planned Pearl Harbor.* New York: McGraw-Hill, 1990.

Kimmett, Larry and Margaret Regis. *The Attack on Pearl Harbor.* Seattle, WA: Navigator Publishing, 1991.

Lambert, John W. and Norman Polmar. *Defenseless: Command Failure at Pearl Harbor.* St. Paul, MN: Motorbooks International, 2003.

Prange, Gordon W. with Daniel M. Goldstein and Katherine V. Dillon. *At Dawn We Slept: The Untold Story of Pearl Harbor.* New York: Penguin Books, 1981.

Prange, Gordon. *God's Samurai: Lead Pilot at Pearl Harbor.* New York: Brassey's, 1990.

Smith, Carl. *Pearl Harbor 1941—The Day of Infamy.* Rev. ed. New York: Osprey Publishing, 2011.

Shinsato, Douglas T. *101 Lesser Known Facts Related to the Attack on Pearl Harbor.* Kameula, HI: eXperience, 2013.

Shinsato, Douglas T. and Tadanori Urabe, trans. *For That One Day: The Memoirs of Mitsuo Fuchida, Commander of the Attack on Pearl Harbor.* Kameula, HI: eXperience, 2011.

Stille, Mark. *Tora! Tora! Tora!—Pearl Harbor 1941.* New York: Osprey Publishing, 2011.

Stillwell, Paul. *Air Raid: Pearl Harbor! Recollections of a Day of Infamy.* Annapolis, MD: Naval Institute Press, 1981.

________. *Battleship Arizona: An Illustrated History.* Annapolis, MD: Naval Institute Press, 1991.

Van Der Vat, Dan. *Pearl Harbor: The Day of Infamy—An Illustrated History.* Toronto: Madison Press Books, 2001.

Willmott, H. P. *Pearl Harbor.* London: Cassell & Co., 2001.

ABOUT THE AUTHORS

Daniel Martinez, M.P.A., is a U.S. National Park Service Ranger and chief historian at the USS *Arizona* and World War II Valor in the Pacific National Monument at Pearl Harbor. He also serves as an adjunct professor at the U.S. Naval War College. From 2002 to 2006, he was the creator, host, and historian in-residence for the Discovery Channel series, "Unsolved History." He also worked on several Discovery Channel documentaries, including "*Arizona*: Death of a Battleship."

Timothy J. Demy, Ph.D., is a professor at the U.S. Naval War College. He previously served as an officer in the U.S. Navy for 27 years. He is the author and co-author of numerous books and articles on a variety of topics in military history, ethics, religion, and security.